5.00

D0338086

∽SPURGEON∽

The Power of Prayer in a Believer's Life

∾∽

CHRISTIAN∽LIVING∽CLASSICS

CHARLES SPURGEON
CHRISTIAN LIVING CLASSICS

Grace Abounding in a Believer's Life

A Passion for Holiness in a Believer's Life

The Power of Prayer in a Believer's Life

Spiritual Warfare in a Believer's Life

The Triumph of Faith in a Believer's Life

What the Holy Spirit Does in a Believer's Life

CHARLES SPURGEON

Christian Living Classics

The Power of Prayer in a Believer's Life

Compiled and Edited by ROBERT HALL

Emerald Books

P.O. Box 635 • Lynnwood, Washington 98046

THE POWER OF PRAYER IN A BELIEVER'S LIFE
Copyright © 1993
Lance C. Wubbels
All Rights Reserved

ISBN 1-883002-03-6

Published by Emerald Books
P.O. box 635
Lynnwood, Washington 98046

Printed in the United States of America

To My Daughter

Ingerlisa

"For what is our hope or joy
or crown of boasting
before our Lord Jesus at his coming?
Is it not you?
For you are our glory and joy."

About the Editor

ROBERT HALL is the pseudonym for Lance Wubbels, the managing editor of Bethany House Publishers. His interest in the writings of Charles Spurgeon began while doing research on an editorial project that required extensive reading of Spurgeon's sermons. He discovered a wealth of sermon classics that are filled with practical, biblical insight for every believer and written in a timeless manner that makes them as relevant today as the day they were spoken. His desire is to select and present Spurgeon's writings in a way that will appeal to a wide audience of readers and allow one of the greatest preachers of all time to enrich believers' lives.

About the Author

CHARLES HADDON SPURGEON (1834–1892) was the remarkable British "Boy Preacher of the Fens" who became one of the truly greatest preachers of all time. Coming from a flourishing country pastorate in 1854, he accepted a call to pastor London's New Park Street Chapel. This building soon proved too small and so work on Spurgeon's Metropolitan Tabernacle was begun in 1859. Meanwhile his weekly sermons were being printed and having a remarkable sale—25,000 copies every week in 1865 and translated into more than twenty languages.

Spurgeon built the Metropolitan Tabernacle into a congregation of over 6,000 and added well over 14,000 members during his thirty-eight-year London ministry. The combination of his clear voice, his mastery of language, his sure grasp of Scripture, and a deep love for Christ produced some of the noblest preaching of any age. An astounding 3,561 sermons have been preserved in sixty-three volumes, *The New Park Street Pulpit* and *The Metropolitan Tabernacle Pulpit*, from which the chapters of this book have been selected and edited.

During his lifetime, Spurgeon is estimated to have preached to 10,000,000 people. He remains history's most widely read preacher. There is more available material written by Spurgeon than by any other Christian author, living or dead. His sixty-three volumes of sermons stand as the largest set of books by a single author in the history of Christianity, comprising the equivalent to the twenty-seven volumes of the ninth edition of the *Encyclopedia Britannica*.

Contents

Introduction

WHEN THE ENGLISH BAPTIST preacher Charles Spurgeon died in January 1892, it was reported that sixty thousand people came to pay homage during the three days his body lay in state at the Metropolitan Tabernacle. A funeral procession two miles long followed his hearse from the Tabernacle to the cemetery at Upper Norwood, and one hundred thousand people stood along the way. London south of the Thames went into mourning—flags flew at half-mast, shops and pubs were closed. It was a remarkable demonstration of affection and respect for the man considered by his peers then and now, "The Prince of Preachers."

A brief study of the early years of this quintessential Victorian Englishman whose masterful preaching astonished his generation makes the accomplishments of Spurgeon's life seem even more remarkable. Spurgeon had none of the advantages of privilege, education, or aristocratic connections that might have paved the way to such a phenomenal ministry. Born the son of Nonconformist ministers, Spurgeon spent much of his childhood in a small agricultural village. Throughout his life, his roots and values remained those of rural, pre-industrial Britain. His formal education, by nineteenth-century standards, was mediocre. He did not seek formal ministerial training, and he did not attend college. When the New Park Street Church in London invited Spurgeon to come preach for a six-month trial period, he asked to come for only three months because "the congregation might not want me, and I do not wish to be a hindrance." Such were his humble beginnings.

One wonders what Charles Spurgeon would say was the secret that gave power to such effective preaching. Several factors have been highlighted by those who have studied Spurgeon's career. Much is made of the combination of a beautiful speaking voice, a dramatic flair and style that was captivating, a powerful commitment to a biblical theology, and his ability to speak to the people of his day in a manner that addressed their deepest needs. Undoubtedly, all of these were of major importance. But they don't explain the most important ingredient.

Lewis Drummond, one of Spurgeon's biographers, has pointed out that foremost of all, Charles Spurgeon was a man of God. The depth and breadth of his spirituality was profound. His earliest memories and heroes were those of the valiant Puritans, such as John Bunyan, who were jailed for their faith and whose godly lives became his model. He often quoted medieval mystics as well as William Law, John Wesley, and other spiritual giants of European Christianity.

And he was devoted to prayer. When people would walk through the Metropolitan Tabernacle, Spurgeon would take them to a basement prayer room where people were always on their knees interceding for the church. Then the pastor would declare, "Here is the powerhouse of this church." Perhaps this best explains the success of Charles Spurgeon. As you read through these chapters, note how often Spurgeon solemnly pled with his own congregation to pray for him. The words of the Apostle Paul, "Brethren, pray for us," were echoed throughout his entire ministry, and the fruit of those prayers is evident.

Out of the astounding index of 3561 Spurgeon sermons that are recorded, it is amazing how many sermons he preached on prayer. A casual study of the sermon titles would indicate well over one hundred sermons on prayer, but closer research would probably easily double that number. Spurgeon was a great believer in passionate, Holy Spirit-directed prayer. His word pictures of the amazing throne of grace that God calls believers to be privileged to come before is well worth the price of the book alone. Yet while Spurgeon was a marvelous encourager in prayer, he knew and spoke about the struggles of prayer that every believer experiences.

I invite you to read these twelve insightful chapters on prayer as you would listen to a trusted and skilled pastor. Carl F. H. Henry wrote of Charles Spurgeon what is so applicable to this theme of prayer: "Multitudes of Christians still draw deeply at the well of Spurgeon's refreshing and victorious messages. The world will stop, look, and listen when it hears such a voice, and it is no surprise that even in the late twentieth century the good this has done lives on to bless our generation."

Careful editing has helped to sharpen the focus of these sermons while retaining the authentic and timeless flavor they undoubtedly bring.

He is the most Holy of all kings. His throne is a great white throne—unspotted and clear as crystal. "The stars are not pure in his sight. How much less man, that is a worm?" (Job 25:5–6). With what lowliness should you draw near to Him. Familiarity there may be, but let it not be unhallowed. Boldness there should be, but let it not be impertinent. You are still on earth, and He in heaven. You are still a worm of the dust, and He the Everlasting. Before the mountains were brought forth, He was God, and if all created things should pass away, yet He would still be the same. I am afraid we do not bow as we should before the Eternal Majesty. Let us ask the Spirit of God to put us in a right frame, that every one of our prayers may be a reverential approach to the Infinite Majesty above.

Chapter One

The Throne of Grace

The throne of grace—Hebrews 4:16.

THESE WORDS ARE FOUND embedded in that gracious verse, "Let us therefore come boldly unto the throne of grace, that we may obtain mercy, and find grace to help in time of need." They are a gem in a golden setting. True prayer is an approach of the soul by the Spirit of God to the throne of God. It is not the utterance of words, it is not alone the feeling of desires, but it is the advance of the desires to God, the spiritual approach of our nature toward the Lord our God. True prayer is neither a mere mental exercise nor a vocal performance. It is far deeper than that—it is spiritual transaction with the Creator of heaven and earth. God is a Spirit unseen of mortal eye and only to be perceived by the inner man. Our spirit within us, begotten by the Holy Ghost at our regeneration, discerns the Great Spirit, communes with Him, presents to Him its requests, and receives from Him answers of peace. True prayer is a spiritual business from beginning to end, and its aim and object end not with man but reach to God Himself.

To qualify for such prayer, the work of the Holy Ghost Himself is needed. If prayer were of the lips alone, we should need only breath in our nostrils to pray. If prayer were of the desires alone, many excellent desires are easily felt, even by natural men. But when prayer is the spiritual desire and fellowship of the human spirit with the Great Spirit, the Holy Ghost Himself must be present all through it—to help our weaknesses and give life and power—or else true prayer will never be presented. The thing offered to God will wear the name and have the form of prayer, but the inner life will be far from it.

It is clear, moreover, from the connection of our text that the mediation of the Lord Jesus Christ is essential to acceptable prayer. As prayer will not be truly prayer without the Spirit of God, so it will not be prevailing prayer without the Son of God. Not only must He, the Great High Priest, go within the veil for us, but through His crucified person, the veil must be entirely taken away. Until then, we are shut out from the living God. The man who, despite the teaching of Scripture, tries to pray without a Savior insults the Deity. The man who imagines that his own natural desires—unsprinkled by the precious blood—will be an acceptable sacrifice before God, makes a mistake. Prayer becomes powerful before the Most High only when it is wrought in us by the Spirit and presented for us by the Christ of God.

My desire is that your soul may be led to come to the Throne of Grace. In addressing the text, I shall bring it to you this way. First, *here is a throne*. Second, *here is grace*. We will then put the two together, and we shall see *grace on a throne*. Putting them together in another order, we shall then see *sovereignty manifesting itself and resplendent in grace*.

Here Is a Throne

"The throne of grace." That God is to be viewed in prayer as our Father is the aspect that is dearest to us. But we still are not to regard Him as though He were such as we are, for our Savior has qualified Our Father with the words "which art in heaven." Close at the heels of that condescending name, to remind us that our Father is still infinitely greater than ourselves, He bids us say, "Hallowed be thy name. Thy kingdom come" (Matt. 6:9–10). Our Father is to be regarded as a King, and in prayer we come, not only to our Father's feet but also to the throne of the Great Monarch of the universe. The mercy seat is a throne, and we must not forget this.

If we should always regard prayer as an entrance into the courts of the royalty of heaven, and if we are to behave ourselves as courtiers in the presence of an illustrious majesty, we are not at a loss to know the right spirit in which to pray. If in prayer we come to a throne, it is clear that our spirit should, in the first place, be one of *lowly reverence*. It is expected that the courtier, in approaching the king, should pay the king homage and honor. The pride that will not acknowledge the king and the treason that rebels against the sovereign should, if it is wise, avoid any near approach to the throne. Let pride bite the curb at a distance, let treason lurk in corners, for only lowly reverence may come before the king himself when he sits clothed in his robes of majesty.

In our case, the King before whom we come is the highest of all monarchs, the King of kings, the Lord of lords. Emperors are but the shadows of our King's imperial power. Some call themselves kings by divine right, but what divine right have they? Common sense laughs their pretensions to scorn. The Lord alone has divine right, and to Him only does the kingdom belong. He is the blessed and only monarch. Nominal kings are set up and put down at the will of men or the decree of providence, but He is Lord alone, the Prince of the kings of the earth.

My heart, be sure that you prostrate yourself in such a presence. If He is so great, place your mouth in the dust before Him, for He is the most powerful of all kings. His throne has sway in all worlds. Heaven obeys Him cheerfully, hell trembles at His frown, and earth is constrained to yield Him worship, willingly or unwillingly. His power can create or destroy. My soul, be sure that when you draw near to the Omnipotent, who is as a consuming fire, put your shoes from off your feet and worship Him with lowliest humility.

He is the most Holy of all kings. His throne is a great white throne—unspotted and clear as crystal. "The stars are not pure in his sight. How much less man, that is a worm?" (Job 25:5–6). With what lowliness should you draw near to Him. Familiarity there may be, but let it not be unhallowed. Boldness there should be, but let it not be impertinent. You are still on earth, and He in heaven. You are still a worm of the dust, and He the Everlasting. Before the mountains were brought forth, He was God, and if all created things should pass away, yet He would still be the same. I am afraid we do not bow as we should before the Eternal Majesty. Let us ask the Spirit of God to put us in a right frame, that every one of our prayers may be a reverential approach to the Infinite Majesty above.

We come to a throne to be approached with *devout joyfulness*. If I find myself favored by divine grace to stand among those favored ones who frequent His courts, shall I not feel glad? I might have been in His prison, but now I am before His throne. I might have been driven from His presence forever, but I am permitted to come even into His royal palace, into His secret chamber of gracious audience. Shall I not then be thankful? Shall not my thankfulness ascend into joy, and shall I not feel that I am made recipient of great favors when I am permitted to pray? Why, then, is your countenance sad when you stand before the throne of grace? If you were before the throne of justice to be condemned for your sins, your hands might well be at your sides. But now that you are favored to come before the King in His silken robes of love, let your face shine with sacred delight. If your sorrows are heavy, tell them to Him, for He can comfort you. If your sins are multiplied, confess them, for He can forgive them. O you courtiers in the halls of such a monarch, be exceedingly glad and mingle praises with your prayers.

Whenever this throne is approached, it should be with *complete submission*. We do not pray to God to instruct Him as to what He should do; neither for a moment must we presume to dictate the method of the divine working. We are permitted to say to God, "Thus we would have it," but we must evermore add, "Yet, seeing that we may be mistaken and are still in the flesh, not as we will, but as You will." Who shall dictate to the throne? No loyal child of God will for a moment imagine that he is to occupy the place of the King, but he bows before Him who has a right to be Lord of all. And though he utters his desire earnestly, passionately, importunately, and he pleads and pleads again, yet it is evermore with this needful reservation: "Your will be done, my Lord; and, if I ask anything that is not in accordance with You, my inmost will is that You would be kind enough to deny me. I will take it as a true answer if You refuse me what does not seem good in Your sight." If we constantly remember this, I think we should be less inclined to push certain concerns before the throne. We should feel, "I am here seeking my own ease, my own comfort, my own advantage, and I may be asking for that which would dishonor God; therefore I will speak with the deepest submission to the divine decrees."

If it is a throne, it should be approached with *enlarged expectations*. We do not come, as it were, in prayer only to where God dispenses His favors to the poor or to the backdoor of the house of mercy to receive the scraps, though that were more than we deserve. To eat the crumbs that fall from the Master's table is more than we could claim. But when we pray, we are standing in the palace, on the glittering floor of the great King's own reception room. In prayer we stand where angels bow with veiled faces. There, even there, the cherubim and seraphim adore before that selfsame throne to which our prayers ascend. And shall we come there with stunted requests and narrow, contracted faith? He is a King who distributes pieces of broad gold, making a sumptuous "feast of fat things, . . . of wines on the lees well refined" (Isa. 25:6). Take heed of imagining that God's thoughts are your thoughts and His ways your ways (Isa. 55:8). Do not bring before God stinted petitions and narrow desires, but remember, as high as the heavens are above the earth, so high are His ways above your ways and His thoughts above your thoughts. Ask, therefore, after a Godlike fashion, for great things, for you are before a great throne. Oh, that we always felt this when we came before the throne of grace, for then He would do for us "exceeding abundantly above all that we ask or think" (Eph. 3:20).

The right spirit in which to approach the throne of grace is that of *unstaggering confidence*. Who shall doubt the King? Who dares question the Imperial word? It was well said that if integrity were banished from the hearts of all mankind, it ought still to dwell in the hearts of kings. Shame on a king if he can lie. The poorest beggar in the streets is dishonored by a broken promise, but what shall we say of a king if his word cannot be depended upon? Shame on us if we are unbelieving before the throne of the King of heaven and earth. With our God before us in all His glory, sitting on the throne of grace, will our hearts dare to say we mistrust Him? Shall we imagine either that He cannot—or will not—keep His promise? Banished be such blasphemous thoughts, and if they must come, let them come upon us when we are somewhere in the outskirts of His dominions—if there is such a place—but not in prayer. When we are in His immediate presence, beholding Him in all the glory of His throne of grace, this surely is the place for the child to trust his Father, for the loyal subject to trust his Monarch. Therefore, take far from the throne all wavering and suspicion. Unstaggering faith should be predominant before the mercy seat.

If prayer is a coming before the throne of God, it should always be conducted with the *deepest sincerity* and in the spirit that makes everything *real*. If you are disloyal enough to despise the King, for your own sake, do not mock Him to His face and when He is upon His throne. If anywhere you dare repeat holy words without heart, let it not be in Jehovah's palace. If a person should ask for an audience with royalty and then should say, "I don't know why I have come or that I have anything in particular to ask," would he not be guilty of folly? As for our great King, when we venture into His presence, let us have a purpose there. Let us beware of playing at praying; it is insolence toward God.

If I am called upon to pray in public, I must not dare to use words that are intended to please the ears of others, but I must realize that I am speaking to God Himself and that I have business to transact with the great Lord. And in my private prayer, if I bow my knee and repeat certain words, I rather sin than do anything that is good, unless my very soul speaks unto the Most High.

Do you think that the King of heaven is delighted to hear you pronounce words with a frivolous tongue and a thoughtless mind? You know Him not. "God is a Spirit: and they that worship him must worship him in spirit and in truth" (John 4:24). If you have any empty forms to prate, go and pour them out into the ears of fools like yourself, but not before the Lord of Hosts. The spiritual God seeks spiritual worshippers, and such He will accept, and only such. "The sacrifice of the wicked is an abomination to the LORD, but the prayer of the upright is his delight" (Prov. 15:8).

The gathering up of all our remarks is just this—prayer is an eminent and elevated act, a high and wondrous privilege. Under the old Persian Empire, a few of the nobility were permitted at any time to come before the king, and this was thought to be the highest privilege possessed by mortals. You and I, the people of God, have permission to come before the throne of heaven at any time we will, and we are encouraged to come there with great boldness.

But let us never forget that it is no small thing to be a courtier in the courts of heaven and earth, to worship Him who made us and sustains us in being. Truly, when we come to pray, we may hear the voice out of the excellent glory saying, "Bow the knee." From all the spirits that behold the face of our Father who is in heaven, even now, I hear a voice that says, "O come, let us worship and bow down: let us kneel before the LORD our Maker. For he is our God, and we are the people of his pasture, and the sheep of his hand. . . . O worship the LORD in the beauty of holiness: fear before him, all the earth" (Ps. 95:6–7; 96:9).

Here Is Grace

Lest the glow and brilliance of the word *throne* should be too much for mortal vision, our text now presents us with the soft, gentle radiance of that delightful word, *grace*. We are called to the throne *of grace*, not to the throne of law. Rocky Sinai once was the throne of law, when God came to Paran with ten thousand of His holy ones. Who dared to draw near to that throne? Even Israel did not. Bounds were set about the mount, and if a beast or man but touched the mount, it was stoned or shot through (Ex. 19:13). To the self-righteous ones who hope they can obey the law and be saved by it, look to the flames that Moses saw, then tremble and despair. To that throne we do not come now, for through Jesus, the case is changed. To a conscience cleansed by the precious blood, there is grace upon the divine throne.

We are not to speak of the throne of ultimate justice. Before God's throne we shall all come, and as many of us as have believed will find it to be a throne of grace as well as of justice. He who sits upon that throne shall pronounce no sentence of condemnation against the man who is justified by faith. The time has not yet arrived when the resurrection trumpet shall ring out so shrill and clear. Not yet do we see the angels with their vengeful swords coming forth to smite the foes of God. Not yet are the great doors of the pit opened to swallow up the enemies who would not have the Son of God to reign over them.

We are still on praying ground and pleading terms with God, and the throne to which we are called to come is the throne of grace. It is a throne set up on purpose for the dispensation of grace and from which every utterance is an utterance of grace. The scepter that is stretched out from it is the silver scepter of grace. The decrees proclaimed from it are purposes of grace. The gifts that are scattered down its golden steps are gifts of grace, and He who sits upon the throne is grace Himself. That it is the throne of grace that we approach when we pray is a mighty source of encouragement to all of us who are praying men and women.

If in prayer I come before a throne of grace, *the faults of my prayer will be overlooked.* In beginning to pray, you may feel as if you did not pray at all. When you rise from your knees, the groanings of your spirit are such that you think there is nothing in them. What a blotted, blurred, smeared prayer it is. Never mind—you did not come to the throne of justice. God does not perceive the fault in the prayer or spurn it. Your broken words, gaspings, and stammerings come before a throne of grace. When any one of us has presented his best prayer before God, if he saw it as God sees it, there is no doubt he would make great lamentation over it. There is enough sin in the best prayer that was ever prayed to secure its being cast away from God.

But the throne is not a throne of justice, and here is the hope for our lame, limping supplications. Our condescending King does not maintain a stately etiquette in His court like those observed by princes among men, where a little mistake or a flaw would secure the petitioner's being dismissed. No, He does not severely criticize the faulty cries of His children. The Lord High Chamberlain of the palace above, our Lord Jesus Christ, takes care to alter and amend every prayer before He presents it to His father. He makes the prayer perfect with His perfection and prevalent with His own merits. God looks upon the prayer as presented through Christ and forgives all its own inherent faultiness. How this should encourage any of us who feel ourselves to be feeble, wandering, and unskillful in prayer! If you cannot plead with God as sometimes you did in years gone by, if you feel as if somehow or other you have grown rusty in the work of supplication, never give up. But come still and come oftener, for it is not a throne of severe criticism to which you come.

Inasmuch as it is a throne of grace, *the faults of the petitioner himself shall not prevent the success of his prayer.* Oh, what faults there are in us! To come before a divine throne with our imperfections—how unfit we are! Dare you think of praying were it not that God's throne is a throne of grace? If you could, I confess I could not. An absolute God, infinitely holy and just, could not in consistency with His divine nature answer any prayer from such a sinner as I am, were it not that He has arranged a plan by which my prayer comes up no longer to a throne of absolute justice. I come to a throne that is also the mercy seat, the propitiation, the place where God meets sinners through Jesus Christ.

I could not say to you, "Pray," not even to you saints, unless it were a throne of grace. But now I will say this to every sinner, though he should think himself to be the worst sinner who ever lived: cry to the Lord and seek Him while He may be found. A throne of grace is a place fitted for you. By simple faith, go to your Savior, for He is the throne of grace. It is in Him that God is able to dispense grace to the most guilty of mankind. Blessed be God, the faults neither of the prayer nor of the suppliant shall shut out our petitions from the God who delights in broken and contrite hearts.

If it is a throne of grace, *the desires of the pleader will be interpreted.* If I cannot find words in which to utter my desires, God in His grace will read my desires without the words. He understands the meaning of His saints, the meaning of their groans. A throne that was not gracious would not trouble itself with our petitions. But God, the infinitely gracious One, will dive into the soul of our desires and read there what we cannot speak with the tongue. Have you never seen the parent who knows very well what it is the little one is trying to say? And so the ever-blessed Spirit, from the throne of grace, will help us and teach us words, even write in our hearts the desires themselves. We have in Scripture instances where God puts words into sinners' mouths. "Take with you words," saith He, "and turn to the LORD: say unto him, . . . receive us graciously" (Hos. 14:2). Take away all iniquity, and He will put the desires and the expression of those desires into your spirit by His grace. He will direct your desires to the things that you ought to seek for. He will teach you your real needs, though as yet you do not know them. He will suggest to you His promises that you may be able to plead them. In fact, He will be the Alpha and Omega to your prayer, just as He is to your salvation. As salvation is from first to last of grace, so the sinner's approach to the throne of grace is of grace from first to last. What comfort is this! Will we not with the greater boldness draw near to this throne, as we search out the sweet meaning of these precious words, "the throne of grace"?

If it is a throne of grace, *all the needs of those who come to it will be supplied*. The King on such a throne will not say, "You must bring Me gifts and sacrifices." It is not a throne for receiving tribute; it is a throne for dispensing gifts. Come, then, you who are poor as poverty itself, having no merits and destitute of virtues and reduced to a beggarly bankruptcy by Adam's fall and your own transgressions. This is not the throne of majesty that supports itself by the taxation of its subjects, but a throne that glorifies itself by streaming forth like a fountain with floods of good things. "Come, buy wine and milk without money and without price" (Isa. 55:1). All the petitioner's needs shall be supplied because it is a throne of grace.

And so, *all the petitioner's miseries shall be compassionated*. When I come to the throne of grace with the burden of my sins, there is One on the throne who felt the burden of sin in ages long gone by and has not forgotten its weight. When I come loaded with sorrow, there is One there who knows all the sorrows to which humanity can be subjected. Am I depressed and distressed? Do I fear that God Himself has forsaken me? There is One upon the throne who said, "My God, my God, why hast thou forsaken me?" (Matt. 27:46). It is a throne from which grace delights to look upon the miseries of mankind with a tender eye—to consider them and to relieve them. Come, then, you who are not only poor but also wretched, whose miseries make you long for death, and yet you dread it. You captive ones, come in your chains; you slaves, come with the irons upon your souls; you who sit in darkness, come forth all blindfolded as you are. The throne of grace will look on you if you cannot look on it and will give to you, though you have nothing to give in return, and will deliver you, though you cannot raise a finger to deliver yourself.

"The throne of grace." The words grow as I turn them over in my mind. It is a most delightful reflection that if I come to the throne of God in prayer, I may feel a thousand defects, but yet there is hope. I usually feel more dissatisfied with my prayers than with anything else I do. I believe it is difficult to pray in public so as to properly conduct the devotions of a large congregation. We sometimes hear persons commended for preaching well, but if any shall be enabled to pray well, there will be an equal gift and a higher grace in it. But suppose in our prayers there are defects of knowledge: it is a throne of grace, and our Father knows that we have need of these things. Suppose there should be defects of faith: He sees our little faith and still does not reject it. He does not in every case measure out His gifts by the degree of our faith but by the sincerity and trueness of faith. And if even there should be grace defects in our spirit and failures in the fervency or humility of the prayer, still, grace overlooks all this, forgives all this, and His merciful hand is stretched out to enrich us according to our needs. This ought to induce many to pray who have not prayed and make us who have been long accustomed to use the consecrated art of prayer to draw near with greater boldness than ever to the throne of grace.

Grace Enthroned

It is a throne, and who sits on it? It is grace personified that is here installed in dignity. Truly, today, grace is on a throne. In the gospel of Jesus Christ grace is the most predominant attribute of God. How comes it to be so exalted? We reply that grace has a throne *by conquest*. Grace came down to earth in the form of the Well-beloved, and it met with sin. Long and sharp was the struggle, and grace appeared to be trampled under foot of sin. But grace at last seized sin and threw it on its own shoulders; and though all but crushed beneath the burden, grace carried sin up to the cross and nailed it there, slew it there, put it to death forever, and triumphed gloriously. For this cause, at this hour, grace sits on a throne because it has conquered human sin, has borne the penalty of human guilt, and overthrown all its enemies.

Grace, moreover, sits on the throne because it has established itself there *by right*. There is no injustice in the grace of God. God is as just when He forgives a believer as when He casts a sinner into hell. I believe that there is as much and as pure a justice in the acceptance of a soul that believes in Christ as there will be in the rejection of those souls who die impenitent and are banished from

Jehovah's presence. The sacrifice of Christ has enabled God to "be just, and the justifier of him which believeth in Jesus" (Rom. 3:26). He who understands the word *substitution* will see that there is nothing due to punitive justice from any believer, seeing that Jesus Christ has paid all the believer's debts. God would be unjust if He did not save those for whom Christ vicariously suffered, for whom His righteousness was provided, and to whom it is imputed. Grace is on the throne by conquest and sits there by right.

Grace is enthroned this day because Christ has finished His work and gone into the heavens. Grace is enthroned *in power*. When we speak of its throne, we mean that it has unlimited might. Grace neither sits on the footstool of God nor stands in the courts of God, but it sits on the throne as the king. This is the dispensation of grace, the year of grace. "Even so might grace reign through righteousness unto eternal life" (Rom 5:21). We live in the era of reigning grace: "Wherefore he is able also to save them to the uttermost that come unto God by him, seeing he ever liveth to make intercession for them" (Heb. 7:25). If you should meet grace as a merchant with treasure in his hand, I would bid you court its friendship—it will enrich you in the hour of poverty. If you should see grace as one of the peers of heaven, highly exalted, I would bid you seek to get its ear. But when grace sits on the throne, I beseech you close in with it at once. It can be no higher, it can be no greater, for it is written "God is love" (1 John 4:16), which is an *alias* for grace. Come and bow before it; come and adore the infinite mercy and grace of God. Doubt not, halt not, hesitate not. Grace is reigning; grace is God; God is love. Oh, that you, seeing grace is thus enthroned, would come and receive it!

Grace is enthroned by conquest, by right, and by power. It is also enthroned *in glory*, for God glories His grace. It is one of His objects now to make His grace illustrious. He delights to show His pardoning grace to those who repent of their sins. He delights to look upon wanderers and restore them, showing His reclaiming grace. He delights to look upon the brokenhearted and comfort them, showing His consoling grace. There is grace to be had of many kinds—or rather the same grace acting in different ways—and God delights to make His grace glorious. There is a rainbow round about the throne like unto an emerald, the emerald of His compassion and love. O happy souls that can believe this, and believing it can come at once and glorify grace by becoming examples of its power.

The Glory of Grace

The mercy seat is a throne. Though grace is there, it is still a throne. Grace does not displace sovereignty, although the attribute of sovereignty is very high and terrible. Sovereignty's light is like a jasper stone, most precious, and like unto a sapphire stone, or, as Ezekiel calls it, "the terrible crystal." Thus saith the King, the Lord of hosts, "I will have mercy on whom I will have mercy, and I will have compassion on whom I will have compassion. . . . O man, who art thou that repliest against God? Shall the thing formed say to him that formed it, Why hast thou made me thus? Hath not the potter power over the clay, of the same lump to make one vessel unto honour, and another unto dishonour?" (Rom. 9:15, 20–21). These are great and terrible words and are not to be answered. He is a King, and He will do as He wills. None shall stay His hand or say to Him, "What are You doing?"

Lest you be downcast by the thought of His sovereignty, I invite you to the text. It is a throne, and there is unquestionable sovereignty. But to every soul that knows how to pray, to every soul that by faith comes to Jesus, the true mercy seat, divine sovereignty wears no dark and terrible aspect but is full of love. If it is a throne of grace, I gather that the sovereignty of God to a believer is always exercised in pure grace. To you who come to God in prayer, the sovereignty always runs thus: "I will have mercy on that sinner, though he does not deserve it. Because I can do as I will with My own, I will bless him, I will make him My child, I will accept him. He shall be Mine in the day when I make up My jewels." On the mercy seat, God never executed sovereignty other than in a way of grace. He reigns, but in this way: "Grace reigns through righteousness unto eternal life" (Rom. 5:21).

On the throne of grace, sovereignty has placed itself under bonds of love. God will do as He wills, but on the mercy seat, He is under bonds of His own making, for He has entered into covenant with Christ, and so into covenant with His chosen. Though God is and ever must be a sovereign, He never will break His covenant nor alter the word that has gone out of His mouth. He cannot be false to a covenant of His own making. When I come to God in Christ, to God on the mercy seat, I need not imagine that by any act of sovereignty God will set aside His covenant. That is impossible.

Moreover, on the throne of grace, God is again bound to us by His promises. The covenant contains in it many gracious promises, exceeding great and precious. "Ask, and it shall be given you; seek, and ye shall find; knock, and it shall be opened unto you" (Matt. 7:7). Until God said that word or a word to that effect, it was at His own option to hear prayer or not, but it is not so now. If true prayer is offered through Jesus Christ, His truth binds Him to hear it. A man may be perfectly free, but the moment he makes a promise, he is not free to break it; and the everlasting God will not break His promise. He delights to fulfill it. He has declared that all His promises "are yea, and in him Amen" (2 Cor. 1:20). For our consolation when we survey God under the high and terrible aspect of a sovereign, we have this to reflect on, that He is under covenant bonds of promise to be faithful to the souls that seek Him. His throne must be a throne of grace to His people.

And sweetest thought of all, every covenant promise has been endorsed and sealed with blood, and far be it from the everlasting God to pour scorn upon the blood of His dear Son. When a king has given a charter to a city, he may before have been absolute, and there may have been nothing to check his prerogatives, but when the city has its charter, it pleads its rights before the king. Even so God has given to His people a charter of untold blessings, bestowing upon them "the sure mercies of David" (Acts 13:34). Very much of the validity of a charter depends upon the signature and the seal, and how sure is the charter of covenant grace. The signature is the handwriting of God Himself, and the seal is the blood of the Only-begotten.

The covenant is ratified with blood, the blood of His own dear Son. It is not possible that we can plead in vain with God when we plead the blood-sealed covenant, ordered in all things and sure. Heaven and earth shall pass away, but the power of the blood of Jesus with God can never fail. It speaks when we are silent, and it prevails when we are defeated. Better things than that of Abel does it ask for (Heb. 12:24), and its cry is heard. Let us come boldly, for we bear the promise in our hearts.

Prayer comes spontaneously from those who abide in Jesus. Prayer is the natural outgushing of a soul in communion with Jesus. As the leaf and fruit come out of the vine branch without any conscious effort and simply because of its living union with the stem, so prayer buds and blossoms and fruits out of souls abiding in Jesus. As stars shine, so do abiders pray. They do not say to themselves, "It is the time for us to get to our task and pray." No, they pray as wise men eat—namely, when the desire for it is upon them. They do not cry out as under bondage, "At this time I ought to be in prayer, but I do not feel like it. What a weariness it is!" They have a glad errand at the mercy seat and rejoice to go there. Hearts abiding in Christ send forth supplications as fires send out flames and sparks. Souls abiding in Jesus open the day with prayer; prayer surrounds them as an atmosphere all day long; at night they fall asleep praying. They are able joyfully to say, "When I awake, I am still with thee" (Ps. 139:18).

Chapter Two

The Secret of Power in Prayer

*If ye abide in me, and my words abide in you, ye shall ask what ye will, and it shall be done unto you—*John 15:7.

THE GIFTS OF GRACE are not enjoyed all at once by believers. Coming to Christ, we are saved by a true union with Him, but it is by abiding in that union that we further receive the purity, the joy, the power, and the blessedness that are stored up in Christ for His people. See how our Lord states this when He speaks to the believing Jews in the eighth chapter of John: "Then said Jesus to those Jews which believed on him, If ye continue in my word, then are ye my disciples indeed; And ye shall know the truth, and the truth shall make you free" (vss. 31–33).

We do not know all the truth at once: we learn it by abiding in Jesus. Perseverance in grace is an educational process by which we learn the truth fully. The emancipating power of that truth is also gradually perceived and enjoyed. "The truth shall make you free." One bond after another snaps, and we are free indeed. You who are beginners in the divine life may be cheered to know that there is something better still for you: you have not yet received the full reward of your faith. You shall have happier views of heavenly things as you climb the hill of spiritual experience. As you abide in Christ you shall have firmer confidence, richer joy, greater stability, more communion with Jesus, and greater delight in the Lord your God. As physical infancy is beset with many evils from which adulthood is exempt, so it is in the spiritual world.

There are degrees of spiritual attainment among believers, and the Savior here encourages us to reach a certain privilege position that is not for all who say that they are in Christ. He specifies this group as those who are *abiders* in Him. Every believer should be an abider, but many have hardly earned the name as yet. Jesus says, "If ye abide in me, and my words abide in you, ye shall ask what ye will, and it shall be done unto you." You have to live with Christ to know Him, and the longer you live with Him, the more you will admire and adore Him. Yes, and the more you will receive from Him, even grace for grace. Truly He is a blessed Christ to one who is but a month old in grace; but these babes can hardly tell what a precious Jesus He is to those whose acquaintance with Him covers well-nigh half a century! Jesus, in the esteem of abiding believers, grows sweeter and dearer, fairer and more lovely, day by day. Not that He improves in Himself, for He is perfect. But as we increase in our knowledge of Him, we appreciate more thoroughly His matchless excellences. How glowingly do His old acquaintances exclaim, "He is altogether lovely!" Oh, that we may continue to grow up into Him in all things who is our Head and prize Him more and more!

Power in prayer is the focus of our text and is considered through three questions. First, *what is this special blessing?* "Ye shall ask what ye will, and it shall be done unto you." Second, *how is this special blessing obtained?* "If ye abide in me, and my words abide in you." Third, *why is it obtained in this way?* There are reasons for the conditions laid down as needful to obtaining the promised power in prayer. I trust that the anointing of the Holy Spirit will add to this subject to make it very profitable.

What Is This Special Blessing?

Read the verse again. Jesus says, "If ye abide in me, and my words abide in you, ye shall ask what ye will, and it shall be done unto you."

Observe that our Lord had been warning us that severed from

Him, we can do nothing, and, therefore, we might have expected that He would now show us how we can do all spiritual acts. The text does not run as we might have expected. The Lord Jesus does not say, "Without me ye can do nothing," or, "if ye abide in me, and my words abide in you, ye shall do all spiritual things." He speaks not of what they should themselves be enabled to do but of what should be done to them—"it shall be done unto you." He does not say, "Strength shall be given you sufficient for all those holy doings of which you are incapable apart from me." That would have been true enough, but our most wise Lord improves upon all parallelisms of speech and upon all expectancies of heart, saying something better still. He does not say, "Ye shall do spiritual things," but, "ye shall ask." By prayer you shall be enabled to do, but before all attempts to do, "Ye shall ask." The choice privilege specified is a mighty prevailing prayerfulness. Power in prayer is very much the gauge of our spiritual condition. When that is secured to us in a high degree, we are favored as to all other matters.

One of the first results of our abiding union with Christ will be *the certain exercise of prayer*: "ye shall ask." If others do not seek or knock or ask, you shall. Those who keep away from Jesus do not pray. Those in whom communion with Christ is suspended feel as if they could not pray, but Jesus says, "If ye abide in me, and my words abide in you, ye shall ask." Prayer comes spontaneously from those who abide in Jesus. Prayer is the natural outgushing of a soul in communion with Jesus. As the leaf and fruit come out of the vine branch without any conscious effort and simply because of its living union with the stem, so prayer buds and blossoms and fruits out of souls abiding in Jesus. As stars shine, so do abiders pray. They do not say to themselves, "It is the time for us to get to our task and pray." No, they pray as wise men eat—namely, when the desire for it is upon them. They do not cry out as under bondage, "At this time I ought to be in prayer, but I do not feel like it. What a weariness it is!" They have a glad errand at the mercy seat and rejoice to go there. Hearts abiding in Christ send forth supplications as fires send out flames and sparks. Souls abiding in Jesus open the day with prayer; prayer surrounds them as an atmosphere all day long; at night they fall asleep praying. They are able joyfully to say, "When I awake, I am still with thee" (Ps. 139:18). Habitual asking comes out of abiding in Christ. You will not need to be urged to pray when you are abiding with Jesus. He says, "Ye shall ask," and depend upon it, you will.

You shall also feel most powerfully *the necessity of prayer*. Your great need of prayer will be vividly seen. When we abide in Christ, we feel more than ever that we must ask for more grace. He who knows Christ best knows his own necessities best. He who is most conscious of life in Christ is also most convinced of his own death apart from Christ. He who most clearly discerns the perfect character of Jesus will be most urgent in prayer for grace to grow like Him. The more I seek to be in my Lord, the more I desire to obtain from Him, since I know that all that is in Him is put there on purpose that I may receive it. "And of his fulness have all we received, and grace for grace" (John 1:16). It is just in proportion as we are linked to Christ's fullness that we feel the necessity of drawing from it by constant prayer.

Nobody needs to prove to an abider in Christ the doctrine of prayer, for we enjoy the thing itself. Prayer is now as much a necessity of our spiritual life as breath is of our natural life. We cannot live without asking favors of the Lord. "If ye abide in me, and my words abide in you, ye *shall* ask," and you shall not wish to cease from asking. He has said, "Seek ye my face," and your heart will answer, "Thy face, LORD, will I seek" (Ps. 27:8).

The fruit of our abiding not only is the exercise of prayer and a sense of the necessity of prayer but also includes *liberty in prayer*: "ye shall ask what ye will." Have you not been on your knees at times without power to pray? Have you not felt that you could not plead as you desired? You wanted to pray, but the waters were frozen and would not flow. The will was present, but not the freedom to present that will in prayer. Do you, then, desire liberty in prayer so that you may speak with God as a man speaks with his friend? Here is the way to it: "If ye abide in me, and my words abide in you, ye shall ask what ye will." I do not mean that you will gain liberty as to a mere fluency of words, for that is a very inferior gift. Fluency is a questionable endowment, especially when it is not accompanied with the weight of thought and depth of feeling. Some brethren pray by the yard, but true prayer is measured by weight—not by length. A single groan before God may have more fullness of prayer in it than a fine oration of great length.

He who dwells with God in Christ Jesus is the man whose steps are enlarged in intercession. He comes boldly because he abides at the throne. He sees the golden scepter stretched out and hears the King saying, "Whatsoever ye shall ask in prayer, believing, ye shall receive" (Matt. 21:22). It is the man who abides in conscious union with his Lord who has freedom of access in prayer. Well may he come to Christ readily, for he is in Christ and abides there. Do not attempt to seize this holy liberty by excitement or presumption. There is only one way of really gaining it: "If ye abide in me, and my words abide in you, ye shall ask what ye will." By this means alone shall you be enabled to open your mouth wide, that God may fill it. Thus shall you become Israels and as princes have power with God.

This is not all: the favored man has the privilege of *successful prayer.* "Ye shall ask what ye will, and it shall be done unto you." You may not do it, but it shall be done *unto you.* You long to bear fruit: ask, and it shall be done unto you. Look at the vine branch. It simply remains in the vine, and by remaining in the vine, the fruit comes from it—it is done unto it. Brother and sister in Christ, the purpose for your being, your life's one object and design, is to bring forth fruit to the glory of the Father. To gain this end, you must abide in Christ, as the branch abides in the vine. This is the method by which your prayer for fruitfulness will become successful: "it shall be done unto you." You shall have wonderful prevalence with God in prayer, inasmuch as before you call He will answer, and while you are yet speaking He will hear. "The desire of the righteous shall be granted" (Prov. 10:24). To the same effect is the other text: "Delight thyself also in the LORD; and he shall give thee the desires of thine heart" (Ps. 37:4). There is a great breadth in this text, "Ye shall ask what ye will, and it shall be done unto you." The Lord gives the abider a signed check and permits him to fill in the amount as he wills.

Does the text mean what it says? I never knew my Lord to say anything He did not mean. I am sure that He may sometimes mean more than we understand Him to say, but He never means less. Mind you, He does not say to all men, "I will give you whatever you ask." That would be an unkind kindness. But He speaks to His disciples who have already received great grace at His hands. It is to disciples He commits this marvelous power of prayer. If I may covet earnestly one thing above every other, it is that I may be able to ask what I will of the Lord and have it. The prevailer in prayer is the man to preach successfully, for he may well prevail with man for God when he has already prevailed with God for men. This is the man to face the difficulties of business life, for what can baffle him when he can take everything to God in prayer? One such believer as this in a church is worth ten thousand of us common people. These are the men in whom is fulfilled God's purpose concerning man, whom He made to have dominion over all the works of His hands. The stamp of sovereignty is on the brows of these men, who shape the history of nations and guide the current of events through their power on high. We see Jesus with all things put under Him by the divine purpose, and as we rise into that image, we also are clothed with dominion and are made kings and priests unto God. Behold Elijah, with the keys of the rain swinging at his side. He shuts or opens the windows of heaven! There are such men still alive. Aspire to be such men and women that to you the text may be fulfilled: "Ye shall ask what ye will, and it shall be done unto you."

The text seems to imply the possibility of a gift of *continual prayer*: "Ye shall ask"—you shall always ask; you shall never get beyond asking; but you shall ask successfully, for "ye shall ask what ye will, and it shall be done unto you." It is not just upon a few special occasions that you shall pray prevailingly, but you shall possess this power with God so long as you abide in Christ and His words abide in you. God will put His omnipotence at your disposal, putting forth His Godhead to fulfill the desires that His own Spirit has worked into your life. I wish I could make this jewel glitter before the eyes of all the saints until they cried out, "Oh, that we had it!" This power in prayer is like the sword of Goliath— wisely may every David say, "There is none like it. Give it to me." This weapon of all-prayer beats the enemy and at the same time enriches its possessor with all the wealth of God. How can he lack anything to whom the Lord has said, "Ask what ye will, and it shall be done unto you"? Come, let us seek this privilege of mighty prayerfulness. Listen, and learn the way. Follow now, while by the light of the text I point out the path. May the Lord lead us into it by His Holy Spirit!

How Is It to Be Obtained?

Here are the two feet by which we climb to power with God in prayer. The first line tells us that we are to *abide in Christ Jesus our Lord*. It is taken for granted that we are already in Him. As believers we are to remain tenaciously clinging to Jesus, lovingly knit to Jesus. We abide in Him by always trusting Him—and Him only— with the same simple faith that joined us to Him at the first. We must never admit any other thing or person into our heart's confidence as our hope of salvation, but we must rest alone in Jesus as we received Him at the first. His Godhead, His manhood, His life, His death, His resurrection, His glory at the right hand of the Father—in a word, Himself—must be our heart's sole reliance. This is absolutely essential. A temporary faith will not save—an abiding faith is needed.

Abiding in the Lord Jesus not only means trusting in Him. It also includes our yielding ourselves to Him to receive His life and to let that life work out its results in us. We live *in* Him, *by* Him, *for* Him, *to* Him,, when we abide in Him. We feel that all our separate life has gone: "For ye are dead, and your life is hid with Christ in God" (Col. 3:3). If we move away from Jesus, we become like withered branches fit only to be cast into the fire. We have no reason for existence except that which we find in Christ—and what a marvelous reason that is! The vine needs the branch as truly as the branch needs the vine. No vine ever bore any fruit except upon its branches. Truly it bears all the branches, and so bears all the fruit, but it is by the branch that the vine displays its fruitfulness. Thus are abiding believers needful to the fulfillment of their Lord's design. What a wonderful truth: the saints are needful to their Savior! The church is "his body, the fulness of him that filleth all in all" (Eph. 1:23).

I want you to understand your blessed responsibility, your practical obligation to bring forth fruit, that the Lord Jesus may be glorified in you. Abide in Him. Never remove your consecration to His honor and glory. Never dream of being your own master. Refuse to be the servant of men, but abide in Christ. Let Him be your object as well as the source of your existence. If you get there and stop there in perpetual communion with your Lord, you will soon realize a joy, a delight, a power in prayer such as you never knew before. There are times when we are conscious that we are in Christ, and we know the joy and the peace of fellowship with Him. Let us abide there. Let that blessed sinking of yourself into His life, the spending of all your powers for Jesus, and the firm faith of your union with Him remain in you evermore. Oh, that we might attain to this by the Holy Ghost!

As if to help us understand this, our gracious Lord has given us a delightful parable. Let us look through this discourse of the vine and its branches (John 15:1–17). Jesus says, "Every branch in me that beareth fruit, he purgeth it" (vs. 2). Take care that you *abide in Christ when you are being pruned*. A brother says, "Since I became a Christian, I have had more troubles than ever. Men ridicule me, the devil tempts me, and my business affairs have gone wrong." If you are to have power in prayer, you must take care that you abide in Christ even when the sharp knife is cutting everything away. Endure trials and never dream of giving up your faith because of them. Say, "Though he slay me, yet will I trust in him" (Job 13:15). Your Lord warned that when you first came into the vine you would have to be pruned and cut closely. If you are now feeling the pruning process, you must not think that some strange thing has happened to you. Rebel not because of anything you may have to suffer from the dear hand of your heavenly Father, who is the vinedresser. Cling to Jesus all the more closely. Say, "Cut, Lord, cut if You must. I will cling to You. To whom shall we go? You have the words of eternal life." Yes, cling to Jesus when the pruning knife is in His hand, and so shall ye "ask what ye will, and it shall be done unto you."

Take care also that *when the pruning operation has been carried out, you still cling to your Lord*. Notice the third and fourth verses: "Now ye are clean through the word which I have spoken unto you. Abide in me, and I in you." Abide after cleansing where you were before cleansing. When you are sanctified, abide where you were when first justified. When you see the work of the Spirit increasing in you, do not let the devil tempt you to boast that now you are somebody and need not come to Jesus as a poor sinner. Always rest in His precious blood alone for salvation. Abide still in Jesus. As you kept to Him when the knife cut you, keep to Him now that the tender grapes begin to form. Do not say to yourself,

"What a fruitful branch I am! How greatly I adorn the vine!" You are nothing and nobody. Only as you abide in Christ are you one whit better than the waste wood that is burned in the fire. Yes, we grow, but we abide. We never go an inch farther than abiding in Him, or if not, we are cast forth and wither. Our whole hope lies in Jesus at our best times as well as at our worst. Jesus says, "Now ye are clean through the word which I have spoken unto you. Abide in me, and I in you."

Abide in Christ *as to all your fruitfulness.* "As the branch cannot bear fruit of itself, except it abide in the vine; no more can ye, except ye abide in me" (John 15:4). "Finally, I have something to do," cries one. Certainly you have, but not apart from Jesus. The branch has to bear fruit, but if the branch imagines that it is going to produce a cluster or even a grape by itself, it is utterly mistaken. The fruit of the branch comes through the stem. Your work for Christ must be Christ's work in you or else it will be good for nothing. Your Sunday-school teaching, your preaching, or whatever you do, must be done in Christ Jesus. Not by your natural talent or by plans of your own inventing can you save men. Beware of homemade schemes. Do for Jesus what Jesus bids you do. Remember that our work for Christ—as we call it—must be Christ's work first if it is to be accepted of Him. Abide in Him as to your fruit bearing.

Abide in Him *as to your very life.* Do not say, "I have been a Christian man now twenty years and can do without continued dependence upon Christ." You could not do without Him if you were as old as Methuselah. Your very being as a Christian depends upon your still clinging, still trusting, still depending. This He must give you, for it all comes from Him and Him alone. To sum it all up, if you want that splendid power in prayer, you must remain in loving, living, lasting, conscious, practical, abiding union with the Lord Jesus Christ.

There is a second qualification mentioned in the text that you must not forget: *"and my words abide in you."* How important, then, are Christ's words! He said in the fourth verse, "Abide in me, and I in you," and now as a parallel to this it is, "If ye abide in me, and my words abide in you." Are Christ's words and Christ identical? Yes, practically speaking. Some talk about Christ being the Master, but as to doctrine, they do not care what His Word declares. So long as their hearts are right toward His person, they claim liberty of thought.

We cannot separate Christ from the Word. In the first place, He is the Word. In the next place, how dare we call Him Master and Lord and not do the things that He says, rejecting the truth He teaches? We must obey His precepts or He will not accept us as disciples. Especially that precept of love that is the essence of all His words. We must love God and our brethren. We must cherish love to all men and seek their good. Anger and malice must be far from us. We must walk even as He walked. If Christ's words do not abide in you—both as to belief and practice—you are not in Christ. Christ and His gospel and His commands are one. If you will not have Christ and His words, neither will He have you or your words.

Oh, for grace to pass through these two golden doors! "If ye abide in me, and my words abide in you." Push through the two, and enter into this large room: "Ye shall ask what ye will, and it shall be done unto you."

Why This Privilege Should Be So Obtained?

Why is this extraordinary power of prayer given to those who abide in Christ? May I encourage you to make the glorious attempt to win this pearl of great price! Why is it that by abiding in Christ and having His words abide in us, we get this liberty and prevalence in prayer?

First, *because of the fullness of Christ.* You may very well ask what you will when you abide in Christ, because whatever you may require is already lodged in Him. Do you desire the grace of the Spirit? Go to your Lord's anointing. Do you seek holiness? Go to His example. Do you desire pardon of sin? Look to His blood. Do you need sin to be put to death? Look to His crucifixion. Do you need to be buried to the world? Go to His tomb. Do you want to feel the fullness of a heavenly life? Behold His resurrection. Would you rise above the world? Mark His ascension. Would you contemplate heavenly things? Remember His sitting at the right hand of God and know that He "hath raised us up together, and made us sit together in heavenly places in Christ Jesus" (Eph. 2:6).

I see clearly why the branch gets all it wants while it abides in the stem, since all it wants is already in the stem and is placed there for the sake of the branch. Does the branch want more than the stem can give it? If it did want more, it could not get it, because it has no other means of living but by sucking its life out of the stem. O my precious Lord, if I want anything that is not in You, I desire always to be without it. I desire to be denied a wish that wanders outside of Yourself. But if the supply of my desire is already in You, why should I go elsewhere? You are my all; where else should I look? "For it pleased the Father that in him should all fulness dwell" (Col. 1:19), and the good pleasure of the Father is our good pleasure also. We are glad to draw everything from Jesus. We feel sure that, ask what we will, we shall have it, since He has it ready for us.

The next reason for this is *the richness of the Word of God*. Catch this thought: "If my words abide in you, ye shall ask what ye will, and it shall be done unto you." The best praying man is the man who is most believingly familiar with the promises of God. After all, prayer is nothing but taking God's promises to Him and saying, "Do as You have said." Prayer is the promise utilized. Prayer not based on a promise has no true foundation. If I go to the bank without a check, I need not expect to receive money. It is the "order to pay" that is my power inside the bank and my warrant for expecting to receive.

You who have Christ's words abiding in you are equipped with those things that the Lord regards with attention. If the Word of God abides in you, you can pray because you meet the great God with His own words and thus overcome omnipotence with omnipotence. You put your finger down upon the very lines and say, "Do as You have said." This is the best praying in all the world. So be filled with God's Word. Study what Jesus has said, what the Holy Ghost has left on record in this divinely inspired book, and in proportion as you feed on, retain, and obey the Word in your life, you will be a master in the art of prayer. You have acquired skill as a wrestler with the Covenant Angel in proportion as you can plead the promises of your faithful God. Be well instructed in the doctrines of grace and let the Word of Christ dwell in you richly, that you may know how to prevail at the throne of grace. Abiding in Christ and His words abiding in you are like the right hand and the left hand of Moses being upheld in prayer—Amalek was smitten, Israel was delivered, and God was glorified (Ex. 17:11).

You still may say you do not quite see why a man who abides in Christ should be allowed to ask whatever he wills and it shall be done unto him. I answer again: it is so, because *in such a man as that there is a predominance of grace that causes him to have a renewed will, which is according to the will of God.* Suppose a man of God is in prayer and thinks that something is desirable, yet he remembers that he is nothing but a babe in the presence of his all-wise Father. And so he bows his will and asks as a favor to be taught what to will. Though God bids him ask to what he wills, he shrinks and cries, "My Lord, here is a request that I am not quite clear about. As far as I can judge, it is a desirable thing. But Lord, I am not fit to judge for myself, and therefore I ask You to not give as I will, but as You will." Do you not see that when we are in such a condition as this, our real will is God's will. Deep down in our hearts, we will only what the Lord Himself wills, and what is this but to ask what we will and it is done to us?

It then becomes safe for God to say to the sanctified soul, "Ask what you will, and it shall be done unto you." The heavenly instincts of that man lead him right. The grace that is within his soul thrusts down all covetous lustings and foul desires, and his will is the actual shadow of God's will. The spiritual life is master in him, and so his aspirations are holy, heavenly, Godlike. He has been made a partaker of the divine nature, and as a son is like his father, so now in desire and will he is one with his God. As the echo answers to the voice, so does the renewed heart echo the mind of the Lord. Our desires are reflected beams of the divine will.

You clearly see that the holy God cannot pick up a common man in the street and say to him, "I will give you whatsoever you will." What would such a man ask for? He would ask for a good drink or something else to fulfill an evil lust. It would be very unsafe to trust most men with this permit. But when the Lord has taken a man, has made him new, and has formed him in the image of His dear Son, then He can trust him! Behold, the great Father treats us in our measure as He treats His Firstborn. Jesus could say, "I knew that thou hearest me always" (John 11:42), and the Lord is educating us to the selfsame assurance. We can say with one of old, "My God will hear me." Do not your hearts long to get at this privilege? It is by the way of holiness, the way of union to Christ, the way of a permanent abiding in Him and an obedient holding fast of His truth that you are to come to this privilege. Behold the only safe and true way. When once that way is really trodden, it is a most sure and effectual way of gaining substantial power in prayer.

A man will succeed in prayer *when his faith is strong*, and this is the case with those who abide in Jesus. It is faith that prevails in prayer. The real eloquence of prayer is a believing desire. "All things are possible to him that believeth" (Mark 9:23). A man abiding in Christ with Christ's words abiding in Him is eminently a believer and, consequently, eminently successful in prayer. He has strong faith indeed, for his faith has brought him into vital contact with Christ, and he is therefore at the source of every blessing and may drink to his full at the well itself.

Such a man will also possess *the indwelling of the Spirit of God*. If we abide in Christ and His words abide in us, the Holy Ghost has come and taken up His residence in us. And what better help in prayer can we have? Is it not a wonderful thing that the Holy Ghost makes intercession for the saints according to the will of God? He "maketh intercession for us with groanings which cannot be uttered" (Rom. 8:26).

The Spirit of God knows the mind of God, and He works in us to will what God wills so that a believing man's prayer is God's purpose reflected in the soul as in a mirror. The eternal decrees of God project their shadows over the hearts of godly men in the form of prayer. What God intends to do He tells His servants by inclining them to ask Him to do what He Himself is resolved to do. God says, "I will do this and that"; but then He adds, "For this will I be inquired of by the house of Israel to do it for them." How clear it is that if we abide in Christ, we may ask what we will! For we shall only ask what the Spirit of God moves us to ask, and it is impossible that God the Holy Ghost and God the Father should be at cross-purposes with one another. What the one prompts us to ask, the other has assuredly determined to bestow.

Do you know that when we abide in Christ and His words abide in us, the Father looks upon us with the same eye that He looks upon His dear Son? Christ is the vine, and the vine includes the branches. The branches are a part of the vine. God therefore looks upon us as part of Christ—members of His body, of His flesh and bones. Such is the Father's love to Jesus that He denies Him nothing. Jesus was obedient to death, even the death of the cross; therefore, His Father loves Him as the God-man Mediator, and He will grant Him all His petitions. Is it so that when you and I are in real union with Christ, the Lord God looks upon us in the same way as He looks on Jesus and says to us, "I will deny you nothing; ye shall ask what ye will, and it shall be done unto you"? This is how I understand the text.

I call your attention to one fact that should not be missed: "As the Father hath loved me, so have I loved you" (John 15:9). The same love that God gives to His Son the Son gives to us, and therefore we are dwellers in the love of the Father and of the Son. How can our prayers be rejected? Will not infinite love have respect for your petitions? If your prayers speed not at the throne, suspect that there is some sin that hinders them. If you do not abide in Christ, how can you hope to pray successfully? If you pick and choose His words and doubt this and doubt that, how can you hope to have speed at the throne? If you willfully disobey His words, will not this account for failure in prayer? But abide in Christ, take hold of His words, and be altogether His disciple, and He shall hear you. Sitting at Jesus' feet, hearing His words, you may lift up your eyes to His dear face and say, "My Lord, hear me now." He will answer you graciously and say, "I have heard you in a time accepted, and in the day of salvation have I helped you. Ask what you will, and it shall be done unto you." Oh, for power at the mercy seat!

Every believer should try to reach this place of boundless influence. What might a church be if all her members were mighty in prayer! Aspire to be strong in the Lord and to enjoy this exceedingly high privilege. It is within your reach, children of God! Only abide in Christ, and let His words abide in you, and this special privilege will be yours. These are not irksome duties, but they are in themselves a joy. Go in for them with your whole heart, and you shall have this added to you—that you shall ask what you will and it shall be done unto you.

*S*tones are broken only by an earnest use of the hammer, and the stone mason usually goes down on his knees. Use the hammer of diligence and let the knee of prayer be exercised. There is not a stony doctrine in Revelation that is profitable for you to understand that will not fly into shivers under the exercise of prayer and faith. "To have prayed well is to have studied well" was a wise sentence of Luther's. You may force your way through anything with the leverage of prayers. Thoughts and reasonings may be like the steel wedges that may open a way into truth, but prayer is the lever that forces open the iron chest of sacred mystery. The kingdom of heaven still suffers violence, and the violent take it by force. If you take care that you work away with the mighty implement of prayer, nothing can stand against you.

Chapter Three

The Golden Key to Prayer

Call unto me, and I will answer thee, and shew thee great and mighty things, which thou knowest not—Jeremiah 33:3.

SOME OF THE MOST LEARNED works in the world smell of the midnight oil, but the most spiritual and comforting books and sayings of men usually have a fragrance about them of prison-damp. I might quote many examples, but John Bunyan's *Pilgrim's Progress* may suffice. And this good text of ours, all moldy and chill with the prison in which Jeremiah lay, has nevertheless a brightness and a beauty that it might never have had had it not come as a cheering word to the prisoner of the Lord shut up in the court of the prison house. God's people have always found out the best of their God when in the worst of conditions. God is good at all times, but He seems to be at His best when we are at our worst. "How could you bear your long imprisonment so well?" said one to the Landgrave of Hesse, who had been imprisoned for his loyalty to the principles of the Reformation. He replied, "The divine consolations of martyrs were with me." Doubtless God keeps a deeper and strong consolation for those who have to endure exceeding great tribulation from the enmity of man.

Rutherford had a quaint saying that when he was cast into the cellars of affliction, he remembered that the great King always kept His wine there, and he began to seek at once for the wine bottles and to drink of the "wines on the lees well refined" (Isa. 25:6). They who dive in the sea of affliction bring up rare pearls. You know, my companions in affliction, that it is so. You who have suffered through a long physical illness; you who have seen your earthly goods carried away and have been reduced to near poverty; you who have gone to the grave yet seven times till you have feared that your last earthly friend would be borne away by unpitying Death—you have proved that God is faithful and that as your tribulations abound, so your consolations also abound in Christ Jesus. My prayer is that from this text some other prisoners of the Lord may have its joyous promise spoken to their hearts. If by reason of heaviness of spirit you feel shut away from God, may you hear him say as with a soft whisper in your ears and hearts, "Call upon me, and I will answer thee, and shew thee great and mighty things which thou knowest not."

The text naturally splits itself into three distinct particles of truth that we draw instruction from. First, *prayer is commanded*—"Call unto me." Second, *God has promised an answer*—"And I will answer thee." Third, *faith is encouraged*—"And shew thee great and mighty things which thou knowest not."

Prayer Is Commanded

We are not merely counselled and recommended to pray but are commanded to pray. This is great condescension. When a hospital is built, it is considered sufficient that the doors are open to the sick when they need help. But no order is made that the sick *must* enter the hospital's care. It is thought to be enough to offer its service without issuing a mandate that men *shall* accept it. So it comes as strange that when prayer is concerned, man needs a command to be merciful to his own soul. So marvelous is the condescension of our gracious God that He issues a command of love without which the sons of Adam would rather starve than come partake of the gospel feast.

God's own people need—or else they would not have been given it—a command to pray, because we are very subject to *periods of worldliness*, if indeed that is not our usual state. We do not forget to eat or go to work or go to our beds to rest, but we often do forget to wrestle with God in prayer and spend long periods in consecrated fellowship with our Father and our God. With many believers, the worldly ledger is so bulky that you cannot move it, and the Bible—representing their devotion—is so small that you might almost put it in your coat pocket. Hours for the world! Minutes for Christ! The world has the best, while prayer gets the leftovers of our time. We give our strength and freshness to the ways of mammon and our tiredness to the ways of God. Hence it is that we need to be commanded to attend to that very act that should be our greatest happiness and our highest privilege to perform— to meet with our God. "Call upon me," He says, for He knows that we are apt to forget. "What meanest thou, O sleeper? arise, call upon thy God" (Jonah 1:6) is an exhortation that is needed by us as well as by Jonah in the storm.

God understands what *heavy hearts* we have sometimes, especially when we are under a sense of sin. Satan says to us, "Why should you pray? How can you hope to prevail? In vain you say, 'I will arise and go to my Father,' for you are not worthy to be one of His hired servants. How can you see the King's face after you have played the traitor against Him? How will you dare to approach the altar when you have defiled it, and when the sacrifice that you would bring there is a polluted one?" It is good for us that we are commanded to pray, or else in times of heaviness we might give it up. If God commands me—unfit as I may be—I will creep to the footstool of grace. Since He says, "Pray without ceasing" (1 Thess. 5:17), though my words fail me and my heart itself will wander, yet I will still stammer out the wishes of my hungering soul: "O God, at least teach me to pray and help me to prevail with You."

Are we not commanded to pray also because of our *frequent unbelief*? Unbelief whispers, "What profit is there if you seek the Lord upon this matter? This is a case beyond the list of things wherein God has interposed. If you were in any other position, you might rest upon the mighty arm of God, but here your prayer will not matter. Whether it is too trivial a matter or it is not spiritual enough or it is a matter in which you have sinned too much or it is too high, too hard, too complicated a piece of business, you have no right to bring it before God!" So suggests the foul fiend of hell. Therefore, there stands written as a daily precept suitable to every case into which a Christian can be cast, "Call unto me—call unto me."

Are you sick? "Call unto me, for I am a Great Physician." Are you fearful that you shall not be able to provide for your family? "Call unto me!" Do your children trouble you? "Call unto me." Are your griefs little yet painful, like small points and pricks of thorns? "Call unto me!" Is your burden heavy as though it would make your back break beneath its load? "Call unto me!" "Cast thy burden upon the LORD, and he shall sustain thee: he shall never suffer the righteous to be moved" (Ps. 55:22). In the valley, on the mountain, on the barren rock, beneath the billows in the briny sea, in the furnace when the coals are glowing, in the gates of death when the jaws of hell would shut themselves upon you—never cease to pray, for the commandment addresses you with "Call unto me." Prayer is mighty and will prevail with God to bring you deliverance. These are some of the reasons the privilege of supplication is also spoken of as a duty in the Holy Scripture.

God has given us this command *as His Word that it may be sure and abiding.* You may turn to fifty passages where the same precept is written. I do not often read in Scripture, "Thou shalt not kill" or "Thou shalt not covet." Twice the law is given. But I often read gospel precepts. It may be a timely exercise for some of you to find out how often in Scripture you are told to pray. You will be surprised to find how many times such words as these are given. "And call upon me in the day of trouble: I will deliver thee" (Ps. 50:15). "Ye people, pour out your heart before him" (Ps. 62:8). "Seek ye the LORD while he may be found, call ye upon him while he is near" (Isa. 55:6). "Ask, and it shall be given you; seek, and ye shall find; knock, and it shall be opened unto you" (Matt. 7:7). "Watch and pray, that ye enter not into temptation" (Matt. 26:41). "Pray without ceasing" (1 Thess. 5:7). "Let us therefore come boldly unto the throne of grace" (Heb. 4:16). "Draw nigh to God, and he will draw nigh to you" (James 4:8). "Continue in prayer" (Col. 4:2). I need not multiply where I could not possibly exhaust. I have picked but a few from this great bag of pearls. Come, Christian, you should never question whether you have a right to pray. You should never ask, "May I be permitted to come into His presence?"

When you have so many commands—and God's commands are all promises and all enablings—you may come boldly to the throne of heavenly grace by the new and living way through the rent veil.

But there are times when God commands His people to pray not only in the Bible but also directly *by the motions of His Holy Spirit.* You who know the inner life understand my meaning. You suddenly feel—possibly in the midst of business—the pressing thought that you *must* pray. It may be you do not at first take particular notice of the inclination, but it comes again, and again, and again—"Pray!" I find that in the matter of prayer, I am myself very much like a water wheel that runs well when there is plenty of water but turns with very little force when the brook is growing shallow. It strikes me that whenever our Lord gives you the special inclination to pray, you should double your diligence. Scripture says you ought always to pray and not to faint (Luke 14:1), yet when God gives you the special longing after prayer, you have another command that should compel you to cheerful obedience.

At such times, I think we may stand in the position of David, to whom the Lord said, "When thou hearest the sound of a going in the tops of the mulberry trees, that then thou shalt bestir thyself" (2 Sam. 5:24). That "going in the tops of the mulberry trees" may have been the footfalls of angels hastening to the help of David, who was to smite the Philistines. When God's mercies are coming, their footfalls are our desires to pray. And our desires to pray should be an immediate indication that the set time to favor Zion is come. Sow plentifully now, for you can sow in hope; plow joyously now, for your harvest is sure. Wrestle now, Jacob, for you are about to be made a prevailing prince, and your name shall be called Israel. Now is your time, spiritual merchantmen—the market is high, so trade much and your profit shall be large. See to it that you use the golden hour and reap your harvest while the sun shines. When we enjoy visitations from on high, we should be particularly constant in prayer. If some other less pressing duty comes our way, let it pass. When God bids us specially pray by the motions of His Spirit, we should commit ourselves in prayer.

An Answer Promised

We should never tolerate the ghastly and grievous thought that God will not answer prayer. *His nature*, as manifested in Christ

Jesus, demands it. He has revealed Himself in the gospel as a God of love, full of grace and truth. How can He refuse to help His creatures who humbly seek His face and favor? The story is told that as the Athenian senate met together in the open air, a sparrow that was pursued by a hawk flew in the direction of the senate. Being hard pressed by the bird of prey, the sparrow sought shelter in the bosom of one of the senators. Being a man of rough and vulgar mold, the senator took the bird from his bosom, dashed it on the ground, and so killed it. Whereupon the whole senate rose in uproar and without one single dissenting voice condemned him to die for not rendering aid to a creature that confided in him. Can we suppose that the God of heaven, whose nature is love, could tear out of His bosom the poor fluttering dove that flies from the eagle of justice into the bosom of His mercy? Will He give the invitation to seek His face, and when we with so much trepidation summon courage enough to fly into His bosom, will He then be unjust and ungracious enough to forget to hear our cry and to answer us? Where do such thoughts come from?

Let us recollect, *God's past character* as well as His nature. I mean the character He has won for Himself for His past deeds of grace. Consider that one stupendous display of bounty—"He that spared not his own Son, but delivered him up for us all, how shall he not with him also freely give us all things?" (Rom. 8:32). If the Lord did not refuse to listen to my voice when I was a guilty sinner and an enemy, how can He disregard my cry now that I am justified and saved! How is it that He heard the voice of my misery when my heart knew it not, if after all He will not hear me now that I am His child? The streaming wounds of Jesus are the sure guarantees for answered prayer.

The great gash made near the Savior's heart that let the light into the very depths of the heart of Deity was proof that He who sits in heaven would hear the cry of His people. You misread Calvary if you think that prayer is useless. We have *the Lord's own promise* for it, and He is a God who cannot lie. Has He not said, "Whatsoever ye shall ask in prayer, believing, ye shall receive" (Matt. 21:22). We cannot pray unless we believe: "for he that cometh to God must believe that he is, and that he is a rewarder of them that diligently seek him" (Heb. 11:6). If we have any question at all about whether our prayer will be heard, we are comparable to him who wavers: "For he that wavereth is like a wave of the sea driven with the wind and tossed. For let not that man think that he shall receive anything of the Lord" (James 1:6–7).

Furthermore, *our own experience* leads us to believe that God will answer prayer. I cannot speak for you, but I may speak for myself. If there is anything I know, anything that I am quite assured of beyond all question, it is that praying breath is never spent in vain. My own conversion is the result of long, affectionate, and earnest prayer. Parents prayed for me, God heard their cries, and here I am preaching the gospel. Since then I have adventured upon some things that were far beyond my capacity, but I have never failed because I have cast myself upon the Lord. I have not hesitated to challenge our church with large ideas of what we might do for God, and we have accomplished all that we purposed. I have sought God's help in all my manifold undertakings, and though I cannot tell here the story of my private life in God's work, yet if it were written, it would be a standing proof that there is a God that answers prayer. He has heard *my* prayers—not now and then—so many times that it has grown into a habit with me to spread my case before God with the absolute certainty that whatsoever I ask of God He will give to me. It is not now a perhaps or a possibility. I know that my Lord answers me, and it would be folly to doubt it. I am sure of this, for I have reaped it.

Still remember that prayer is always to be offered in submission to God's will. When we say that God hears prayer, we do not mean that He always gives us literally what we ask for. We do mean, however, that He gives us what is best for us and if He does not give us the mercy we ask for in silver, he bestows it upon us in gold. If He does not take away the thorn in the flesh, yet he says, "My grace is sufficient for thee" (2 Cor. 12:9). We never offer up prayer without inserting the clause, either in spirit or in words, "Nevertheless not as I will, but as thou wilt" (Matt. 26:39). We can only pray without an "if" when we are quite sure that our will must be God's will, because God's will is fully our will.

Encouragement to Faith

"I will shew thee great and mighty things which thou knowest not." Remember that this was originally spoken to a prophet in prison. Therefore, it applies first to *every teacher*. And as every teacher must be a learner, it has a bearing upon *every learner* in divine truth. The best way by which a prophet and teacher and learner can know the higher and more mysterious truths of God is by waiting upon God in prayer. I noticed in reading the book of Daniel, how Daniel came to understand Nebuchadnezzar's dream. The soothsayers, the magicians, and the astrologers of the Chaldees brought out their curious books and their strange-looking instruments, muttering their *abracadabra* and all sorts of mysterious incantations, but they all failed. What did Daniel do? He set himself to prayer, and knowing that the prayer of a united body of men has more prevalence than the prayer of one, we find that Daniel called together his brethren and bade them unite with him in earnest prayer that God in His infinite mercy would be pleased to open up the vision. "Then Daniel went to his house, and made the thing known to Hananiah, Mishael, and Azariah, his companions: That they would desire mercies of the God of heaven concerning this secret; that Daniel and his fellows should not perish with the rest of the wise men of Babylon" (Dan. 2:17–18). And in the case of John (the Daniel of the New Testament), you remember he saw a book in the right hand of Him that sat on the throne—a book sealed with seven seals that none was found worthy to open or to look thereon. What did John do? The book was later opened by the Lion of the Tribe of Judah who had prevailed to open the book, but it is written first before the book was opened, "I wept much" (Rev. 5:4). Yes, and the tears of John which were his liquid prayers were—as far as he was concerned—the sacred keys by which the folded book was opened.

You who are in the ministry or teachers in Sunday school and all of you who are learners in the college of Christ Jesus, I pray you remember that prayer is your best means of study. Like Daniel, you shall understand the dream and its interpretation when you have sought God. And like John, you shall see the seven seals of precious truth unloosed after you have wept much. "Yea, if thou criest after knowledge, and liftest up the voice for understanding; If thou seekest her as silver, and searchest for her as for hid treasures; Then shalt thou understand the fear of the LORD, and find the knowledge of God" (Prov. 2:3–5).

Stones are broken only by an earnest use of the hammer, and

the stone mason usually goes down on his knees. Use the hammer of diligence and let the knee of prayer be exercised. There is not a stony doctrine in Revelation that is profitable for you to understand that will not fly into shivers under the exercise of prayer and faith. "To have prayed well is to have studied well" was a wise sentence of Luther's. You may force your way through anything with the leverage of prayers. Thoughts and reasonings may be like the steel wedges that may open a way into truth, but prayer is the lever that forces open the iron chest of sacred mystery. The kingdom of heaven still suffers violence, and the violent take it by force. If you take care that you work away with the mighty implement of prayer, nothing can stand against you.

We must not, however, stop there. Although we have applied the text to one case, it is applicable to a hundred. We single out another. *The saint may expect to discover deeper experience* and to know more of the higher spiritual life by being much in prayer. There are different translations of the text. One version renders it, "I will shew thee great and fortified things which thou knowest not." Another reads it, "Great and reserved things which thou knowest not." Not all the developments of spiritual life are similarly easy to attain. There are the common frames and feelings of repentance, faith, joy, and hope that are enjoyed by the entire family. But there is an upper realm of rapture, communion, and conscious union with Christ that is far from being the common dwelling place of believers. All believers see Christ, but not all believers put their fingers into the prints of the nails or thrust their hand into His side. Not all of us have the high privilege of John to lean upon Jesus' bosom or to be caught up into the third heaven as Paul was. In the ark of salvation we find a lower, second, and third story—all are in the ark, but not all are in the same story.

Most Christians are only up to their ankles in the river of experience. Some have waded till the stream is up to their knees. A few find the water up to their shoulders. But a very few find it a river to swim in—the bottom of which they cannot touch. There are heights in experiential knowledge of the things of God the eagle's eye of acumen and philosophic thought has never seen. There are secret paths that the lion's cub of reason and judgment has not as yet learned to travel. God alone can bring us there, but the chariot in which He takes us up and the fiery steeds with which that chariot is dragged are prevailing prayers.

Prevailing prayer is victorious over the God of mercy: "By his strength he had power with God: Yea, he had power over the angel, and prevailed: he wept, and made supplication unto him: he found him in Beth-el, and there he spake with us" (Hos. 12:3–4). Prevailing prayer takes the Christian to Carmel and enables him to cover heaven with clouds of blessing and earth with floods of mercy. Prevailing prayer bears the Christ aloft to Pisgah and shows him the inheritance reserved. It elevates him to Tabor and transfigures him, till in the likeness of his Lord, as He is, so are we also in this world. If you would reach to something higher than ordinary experience, look to the Rock that is higher than you, and look with the eye of faith through the windows of importunate prayer. To grow in experience, there must be much prayer.

Allow me to apply this text to two or three more cases. It is certainly true of *the sufferer under trial* that if he waits upon God in prayer, he shall receive greater deliverances than he has ever dreamed of—"Thou drawest near in the day that I called upon thee: thou saidst, Fear not. O LORD, thou hast pleaded the causes of my soul; thou has redeemed my life" (Lam. 3:57–58). And David's is the same: "I called upon the LORD in distress: the Lord answered me, and set me in a large place. . . . I will praise thee: for thou hast heard me, and art become my salvation" (Ps. 118:5, 21). And yet again: "Then they cried unto the LORD in their trouble, and he delivered them out of their distresses. And he led them forth by the right way, that they might go to a city of habitation" (Ps. 107:6–7). "Thy servant my husband is dead," said the poor woman, "and the creditor is come to take unto him my two sons to be bondmen" (2 Kings 4:1). She hoped that Elijah would say, "What are your debts? I will pay them." Instead of that, he multiplies her oil till it is written, "Go, sell the oil,, and pay thy debts, and live thou and thy children of the rest" (2 Kings 4:7).

So often it will happen that God not only helps His people through the miry places of the way but also brings them safely far on the journey. When Jesus Christ came walking upon the stormy sea and the disciples received Him into the ship, not only was the sea calm, but it is recorded: "Immediately the ship was at the land whither they went" (John 6:21). That was a mercy over and above what they asked. I sometimes hear believers pray and make use of a quotation that is not in the Bible: "He is able to do exceeding abundantly above what we *can* ask or even think." I do not know what we can ask or what we can think. But it is said, "Now unto him that is able to do exceeding abundantly above all that we ask or think" (Eph. 3:20). When we are in great trial, let us say, "Now I am in prison. Like Jeremiah, I will pray as he did, for I have God's command to do it; and I will look out as he did, expecting that He will show me reserved mercies that I know nothing of at present." God will not merely bring His people through the battle, but He will bring them forth with banners waving, dividing the spoil with the mighty and claiming their portion with the strong. Expect great things of a God who gives such great promises as these.

Our text is *an encouragement for the Christian worker*. Most believers are doing something for Christ. Wait upon God in prayer, and you have the promise that He will do greater things for you than you know of. We know not how much potential for usefulness may be in us. The ass's jawbone gets into Samson's hands, and what can it *not* do? No one knows what it cannot do now that a Samson wields it. And you have often thought yourself to be as contemptible as that bone, and you have said, "What can I do?" But when Christ by His Spirit grips you, what can you not do? Truly you may adopt Paul's language and say, "I can do all things through Christ which strengtheneth me" (Phil. 4:13). However, do not depend upon prayer without effort. There are many believers who appear to be very mighty in prayer and wondrous in supplication, but then they require God to do what they can do themselves, and therefore, God does nothing at all for them. Listen to the voice of experience and wisdom that says, "Do your best. Work as if all rested upon your toil, as if your own arm would bring your salvation. And when you have done all, cast yourself upon Him without whom it is in vain to rise up early and to sit up late and to eat the bread of carefulness. And if He gives you success, give Him the praise."

This promise ought to prove useful for the comforting of those who are intercessors for others. You who are calling upon God to save your children, to bless your neighbors, to remember your husband or your wife in mercy may take comfort from this—"I will shew thee great and mighty things, which thou knowest not." You cannot guess how greatly God will bless you. Only go and stand at His door, you cannot tell what is in reserve for you. Ruth went to glean and expected to get a few good ears, but Boaz said, "Let her glean even among the sheaves, and reproach her not" (Ruth 2:15). Moreover he said to her, "At mealtime come thou hither, and eat of the bread, and dip thy morsel in the vinegar" (Ruth 2:14). Ruth found a husband where she only expected to find a handful of barley. So in prayer for others, God may give us such mercies that we shall be astounded by them, since we expected so little. Hear what is said of Job and learn its lesson: "My servant Job shall pray for you: for him will I accept: lest I deal with you after your folly, in that ye have not spoken of me the thing which is right, like my servant Job. . . . And the LORD turned the captivity of Job, when he prayed for his friends: also the LORD gave Job twice as much as he had before" (Job 42:8, 10).

I pray you take this text—God Himself speaks it to you: "Call unto me, and I will answer thee, and shew thee great and mighty things, which thou knowest not." At once take God at His Word. Go into your chamber and shut the door and try Him. Try the Lord, prove Him, and see whether He is true or not. If God is true, you cannot seek mercy at His hands through Jesus Christ and get a negative reply. He must—for His own promise and character bind Him to it—open mercy's gate to Jesus, to cry aloud to God, and His answer of peace is already on the way to meet you.

*T*o think that we puny people may speak with God and through God we may move all the worlds. Yet when your prayers are heard, creation will not be disturbed. Though the grandest ends be answered, providence will not be altered for a single moment. Not a leaf will fall earlier from the tree, not a star will stray from its course, nor will one drop of water trickle more slowly from its fount—all will go on the same, and yet your prayers will have affected everything. They will speak to the decrees and purposes of God as they are being daily fulfilled; and the decrees will all shout to your prayer, "You are our brother; we are decrees, and you a prayer; but you are yourself a decree, as old, as sure, as ancient as we are." Our prayers are God's decrees in another shape. The prayers of God's people are but God's promises breathed out of living hearts, and those promises are the decrees, only put into another form and fashion.

Chapter Four

True Prayer—True Power!

Therefore I say unto you, What things soever ye desire, when ye pray, believe that ye receive them, and ye shall have them—Mark 11:24.

THIS VERSE HAS SOMETHING to do with the faith of miracles, but I think it has far more reference to the miracle of faith. I believe that this text is the inheritance not only of the apostles but also of all those who walk in the faith of the apostles, believing in the promises of the Lord Jesus Christ. The advice Christ gave to the twelve and to his immediate followers is repeated to us in God's Word. May we have grace constantly to obey it.

How many people there are who complain that they do not enjoy prayer. They do not neglect it, for they dare not, but they would neglect it if they dared, so far are they from finding any pleasure in prayer. Have we not to lament that often the chariot wheels of prayer are taken off, and we drive on heavily when we are in supplication? We spend the time allotted for prayer, but we rise from our knees unrefreshed. When the time comes round again, conscience drives us to our knees, but there is no sweet fellowship with God. There is no pouring out of our needs to Him in the firm conviction that He will supply them. After repeating a certain round of customary utterances, we rise from our knees perhaps more troubled in conscience and more distressed in mind than we were before. Many Christians complain that they pray, not so much because it is a blessed thing to be allowed to draw near to God, but because they must pray, because it is their duty, because they feel that if they do not, they will lose one of the sure evidences of their being Christians. I do not condemn you if you feel this, but if I may be the means of lifting you up from so low a state of grace into a higher and more healthy atmosphere, my soul shall be exceeding glad. God has a more excellent way for prayer. It is possible for you to come to look at prayer as one of the most delightful exercises of your life. If you shall come to esteem it higher than your necessary food and to value it as one of heaven's best luxuries, surely I shall have answered a great end, and you will have to thank God for a great blessing.

Look at the Text

If you study the verse carefully, I think you will perceive the essential qualities necessary to any great success and prevalence in prayer. According to our Savior's description of prayer, there should always be some *definite objects* for which we plead. He speaks of *things*—"what things soever ye desire." It seems He is implying that God's children would not go to Him in prayer when they have nothing to pray for. Another essential qualification of prayer is *earnest desire*, for the Master clearly states that when we pray we have desires. Unless there is a fullness and overflowing of desires, it is not prayer. It may be something like prayer—the outward form or the bare skeleton—but it is not the living thing, the all-prevailing, almighty thing called prayer.

Observe, too, that *faith* is an essential quality of successful prayer—"believe that ye receive them." You cannot pray so as to be heard in heaven and answered to your soul's satisfaction unless you believe that God really hears and will answer you. One other qualification appears here upon the very surface—namely, that *a realizing expectation* should always go with a firm faith—"believe that ye receive them." Not merely believe that "ye shall," but believe that "ye do" receive them—count them as if they were already received and act as if you had them—act as if you were sure you should have them—"believe that ye receive them, and ye shall have them." Let us review these four qualities, one by one.

To make prayer of any value, *there should be definite objects for which to plead*. We often ramble in our prayers after this, that, and the other, and we get nothing, because in each we do not really desire anything. We chatter about many subjects, but the soul does not concentrate itself upon any one object. Do you not sometimes fall on your knees without first thinking what you mean to ask God for? You do so as a matter of habit, without any motion of your heart. It is like going to a store without knowing what you want to buy. You may perhaps make a good purchase when you are there, but certainly it is not a wise plan to adopt. And so the Christian in prayer may afterward attain to a real desire and get his end, but how much better if, having prepared his soul by consideration and self-examination, he came to God for an object at which he was about to aim with a real request.

We would never consider going into the presence of the Queen of England and then try to think of some petition after we came there. Even so with the child of God, who should be able to answer the great question, "What is your request, and it shall be done for you?" Imagine an archer shooting with his bow and not knowing where the mark is! Would he be likely to have success? Consider a ship on a voyage of discovery, putting out to sea without the captain having any idea of what he was looking for! Would you expect that he would come back heavily laden with either the discoveries of science or treasures of gold? In everything else you have plan. You do not go to work without knowing that there is something that you design to do or make. How is it that you go to God without knowing what you design to have?

If you had some object in mind, you would never find prayer to be dull and tedious. I am persuaded that you would long for it. You would say, "I have something that I want. Oh, that I could draw near to my God and ask Him for it! I have a need, I want to have it satisfied, and I can hardly wait till I can get alone, that I may pour out my heart before Him and ask Him for this great thing after which my soul so earnestly pants." You will find it more helpful to your prayers if you have some objects at which you aim as well as some persons whom you will mention. Do not merely plead with God for sinners in general, but always mention some in particular. If you are a Sunday school teacher, don't simply ask that your class be blessed, but pray for your children by name before the Most High. And if there is a mercy in your household that you crave, be simple and direct in your pleadings with God.

When you pray to Him, tell Him what you want. If you do not have enough money, if you are in tough straits, state the case. Use no mock modesty with God. Come at once to the point and speak honestly with Him. He needs no beautiful oratories such as men will constantly use when they don't like to say right out what they mean. If you need either material or spiritual mercies, say so. Don't ransack the Bible to find words in which to express it. Express your desires in the words that naturally suggest themselves to you. They will be the best words—depend upon it. Abraham's words were the best for Abraham, and yours will be the best for you. You need not study all the texts in Scripture, attempting to pray just as Jacob and Elijah did, using their expressions. If you do, you will imitate them. You may imitate their words, but you lack the soul that suggested and animated their words. Pray in your own words. Speak plainly to God what you want. Name persons, name things, and make a straight aim at the object of your supplications, and I am sure you will soon find that the weariness that you often complain in your intercession will no more fall upon you—or at least not so habitually as it has before.

"But," says one, "I do not feel that I have anything special to pray about." I know not who you are or where you live to be without special concerns for prayer, for I find that every day brings either its need or its trouble that I must tell to my God. But if we are without troubles, have we attained to such a height in grace that we have nothing to ask for? Do we love Christ so much that we have no need to pray that we may love Him more? Have we so much faith that we have ceased to cry, "Lord, increase it"? With a little self-examination, I am sure you will always discover some legitimate object for which you may knock at Mercy's door and cry, "Give me, Lord, the desire of my heart." And if you are without a desire, you have only to ask the first Christian that you meet, and he will tell you of one. "If you have nothing to ask for yourself," he will reply, "pray for me." Ask that a sick wife may be healed. Pray that the Lord would lift up the light of His countenance upon a despondent heart. Ask that the Lord would send help to some minister who has been laboring in vain and spending his strength for so little. When you have finished praying for yourself, plead for others, and if you run out of individuals, look to the huge Sodoms and Gomorrahs that lie around you.

Along with a definite object for prayer, it is equally necessary that there should be *an earnest desire for its attainment.* "Cold prayers," says an old divine, "ask for a denial." When we ask the Lord without passion, we actually stop His hand and restrain Him from giving us the very blessing we pretend that we are seeking. When you have your object in your eye, your soul must become so possessed with the value of that object, with your own excessive need for it, with the danger that you will be in unless that object should be granted, that you will be compelled to plead for it as a man pleads for his life. We must have such a desire for the thing we want that we will not rise until we have it—but in submission to His divine will, nevertheless. Feeling that the thing we ask for cannot be wrong and that He has promised it, we have resolved it must be given, and if not given, we will plead the promise again and again, till heaven's gates shall shake before our pleas shall cease. Oh, those cold-hearted prayers that die upon the lips—those frozen supplications. They do not move men's hearts; how should they move God's heart? They do not come from our own souls or well up from the deep secret springs of our inmost heart, and therefore they cannot rise up to Him who only hears the cry of the soul, before whom hypocrisy can weave no veil or formality practice any disguise. We must be earnest. Otherwise we have no right to hope that the Lord will hear our prayer.

If we comprehended the greatness of the Being before whom we plead, it would restrain all lightness and constrain an unceasing earnestness in prayer. Shall I come into Your presence, O my God, and mock You with cold-hearted words? Do the angels veil their faces before You? Shall I be content to chatter through a form of prayer with no soul and no heart? We little know how many of our prayers are an abomination to the Lord. It would be an abomination to you and me to hear men ask us in the streets as if they did not want what they asked for. But have we not done the same to God? Has not that which is heaven's greatest blessing to man become to us a dry, dead duty? It was said of John Bradford that he had a peculiar art in prayer, and when asked for his secret he said, "When I know what I want, I always stop on that prayer until I feel that I have pleaded it with God, and until God and I have had dealings with each other upon it. I never go on to another petition till I have gone through the first."

Alas, for some believers who begin "Our Father which art in heaven, Hallowed be thy name," before they have realized the adoring—"hallowed be thy name"—they have begun to repeat the next words: "Thy kingdom come." Then perhaps something strikes their mind: "Do I really wish His kingdom to come? If it were to come now, where should I be?" And while they are thinking of that, their voice is going on with, "Thy will be done in earth, as it is in heaven." So they jumble up their prayers and run the sentences together. Stop at each one till you have really prayed it. Do not try to put two arrows on the string at once: they both will miss. Plead once with God and prevail, and then plead again. Get the first mercy, and then go for the second. Do not be satisfied with running the colors of your prayers into one another till there is no picture to look at, but just a huge daub—a smear of colors badly laid on. Look at the Lord's Prayer itself. What clear, sharp outlines it has. There are certain definite mercies, and they do not run into one another. There it stands, and as you look at the whole, it is a magnificent picture—not confusion, but beautiful order. Let it be so with your prayers. Stay on one till you have prevailed with that, and then go on to the next. With definite objects and with fervent desires mixed together, there is the dawning of hope that you shall prevail with God.

A definite object and earnest desire in prayer would not avail if they were not mixed with a still more essential and divine quality—namely, *a firm faith in God.* Do you believe in the power of prayer? There are many Christians who do not. They think prayer is a good thing, and they believe that it sometimes does wonders, but they do not think that prayer—real prayer—is always successful. They think that prayer's effect depends upon many other things, but that it has no essential quality or power in itself. My own soul's conviction is that prayer is the grandest power in the entire universe. It has more omnipotent force than any other force known to mankind. Prayer has as true, as real, as invaluable an influence over the entire universe as any of the laws of matter.

When a man really prays, it is not a question of whether God will hear him or not: He must hear him—not because there is any compulsion in the prayer, but because there is a sweet and blessed compulsion in the promise. God has promised to hear prayer, and He will perform His promise. As He is the Most High and true God, He cannot deny Himself.

To think that we puny people may speak with God and through God we may move all the worlds. Yet when your prayers are heard, creation will not be disturbed. Though the grandest ends be answered, providence will not be altered for a single moment. Not a leaf will fall earlier from the tree, not a star will stray from its course, nor will one drop of water trickle more slowly from its fount—all will go on the same, and yet your prayers will have affected everything. They will speak to the decrees and purposes of God as they are being daily fulfilled; and the decrees will all shout to your prayer, "You are our brother; we are decrees, and you a prayer; but you are yourself a decree, as old, as sure, as ancient as we are." Our prayers are God's decrees in another shape. The prayers of God's people are but God's promises breathed out of living hearts, and those promises are the decrees, only put into another form and fashion. Do not say, "How can my prayers affect the decrees of God?" They cannot, except to the degree that your prayers are decrees, and that as they come out, every prayer that is inspired of the Holy Ghost in your soul is as omnipotent and as eternal as that decree which said, "Let there be light: and there was light" (Gen. 1:3).

You have power in prayer, and you stand among the most potent ministers in the universe that God has made. You have power over angels, who will fly at your will. You have power over fire, and water, and the elements of earth. You have power to make your voice heard beyond the stars. Where the thunders die out in silence, your voice shall wake the echoes of eternity. The ear of God shall listen, and the hand of God shall yield to your will. God bids you cry, "Thy will be done," and your will shall be done. When you can plead His promise, then your will is His will.

What a tremendous thing to have such a power in one's hands as to be able to pray! You have heard sometimes of men who pretended to have a strange power by which to make showers of rain or to stop the sun. It was all a figment of their imagination, but the power of faith in a Christian's life is amazing. If the Christian only has faith in God, there is nothing impossible to him. He shall be delivered out of the deepest waters, rescued out of the sorest troubles, fed in famine, amidst calamity he shall walk firm and strong, and in the day of battle he shall lift up his head, if he can but believe the promise, holding it up before God's eyes and pleading it with the power of unfaltering reliance.

There is no force so tremendous, no energy so marvelous, as the energy with which God has endowed every man, who like Jacob can wrestle and like Israel can prevail with Him in prayer. But we must believe prayer to be what it is, or else it is not what it should be. Unless I believe my prayer to be effectual, it shall not be, for it will depend to a great extent on my faith. God may give me the mercy even when I have no faith. Such is His own sovereign grace, but He has not promised to do it. But when I have faith and can plead the promise with earnest desire, it is no longer a probability as to whether I shall get the blessing or whether my will shall be done. Unless the Eternal will swerve from His Word, unless the oath that He has given shall be revoked and He shall cease to be what He is, "We know that we have the petitions that we desired of him."

And now to mount one step higher. Together with definite objects, fervent desires, and strong faith in the power of prayer, there should be mingled *a realizing expectation*. We should be able to count over the mercies before we have received them, believing that they are on the road. In chapter 10 of the book of Daniel, the whole machinery of prayer seems to be laid bare. Daniel is on his knees in prayer, and a mighty angel comes to him. The angel talks with Daniel and tells him that as soon as Daniel had begun to set his heart to understand the vision he had seen, his words were heard, and the Lord had dispatched the angel. Then the angel tells him in the most businesslike manner in the world, "I should have been here before, but the Prince of Persia withstood me; nevertheless, the prince of your nation helped me, and I have come to comfort and instruct you." See now, God breathes the desire into our hearts, and as soon as the desire is there, before we call, He begins to answer. Before the words have reached halfway to heaven, while they are yet trembling on the lip—knowing the words we mean to speak—He begins to answer them, sends the angel, and brings the needed blessing. Why, the thing is a revelation if you could see it with your eyes.

Some people think that spiritual things are dreams and that we are talking imaginations. I believe there is as much reality in a Christian's prayer as in a lightning flash, and the usefulness and excellency of the prayer of a Christian may be just as sensibly known as the power of the lightning flash when it strikes a tree, breaking off branches and splitting it to the very root. Prayer is not imagination or fiction. It is a real, actual thing, coercing the universe, binding the laws of God themselves in fetters, and constraining the High and Holy One to listen to the will of His poor but favored creature-man. But we need to always believe this. We need a realizing assurance in prayer, counting over the mercies before they arrive! We need to be sure that they are coming and to act as if we have them! When you have asked for your daily bread, take no more care, but believe that God has heard you and will give it to you. When you have taken your sick child before God, believe that the child will recover—or if not, that it will be a greater blessing to you and more glory to God, and so to leave it to Him. To be able to say, "I know He has heard me now. I will look for my God, then hear what He will say to my soul." Were you ever disappointed when you prayed in faith and expected the answer? I bear my own testimony that I have never yet trusted Him and found Him to fail me. I have trusted man and have been deceived, but my God has never once denied the request I have made to Him when I have backed up the request with the sure belief in His willingness to hear and the assurance of His promise.

But I hear someone say, "May we pray for worldly matters?" "In *every thing* by prayer and supplication with thanksgiving let your requests be made known to God" (Phil. 4:6). Prayer is not merely for spiritual but for everyday concerns. Take your smallest trials to Him. He is your household God as well as the God of the sanctuary. Be ever taking all that you have before God. Oh, for more of a sweet habit of spreading everything before the Lord, just as Hezekiah did with Rabshekah's letter (Isa. 37:14), saying, "Your will be done, I leave it to You!" Men say Mr. Muller of Bristol is enthusiastic because he will gather seven hundred children and believe that God will provide for them. Believe me, Muller is not an enthusiast. He is only doing what should be the commonplace action of every Christian. He is acting upon a rule at which the world must always scoff because it does not understand it. It is a system that always appears visionary and romantic to the weak judgment of sense but never appears so to the child of God. Muller acts not upon common sense but upon something higher than common sense—upon uncommon faith. Oh, that we had that uncommon faith to take God at His Word! He cannot and will not permit the man that trusts Him to be ashamed or confounded.

Look About You

Having established what I believe are the four essentials of prevailing prayer, take a look at your prayer meetings and private intercessions and judge them both by the tenor of this text. "What things soever ye desire, when ye pray, believe that ye receive them, and ye shall have them." Look about you at the meetings for prayer. Is it not a fact that as soon as you enter the meeting, you feel that if you are called upon to pray, you have to exercise a gift? And that gift, in the case of many praying men, lies in having a good memory to recall a great many texts that have always been quoted since the days of our grandfather's grandfather. The gift lies also in some churches in having strong lungs so as to be able to pray loud and long without taking a breath for five minutes. The gift lies also in being able to ask for nothing in particular but in passing through a range that covers everything. It makes the prayer like a nondescript machine that has not point whatever, rather than an arrow with a point. It was meant to be all point, aimed at everything, and consequently it strikes nothing. Those brethren are often the most frequently asked to pray who have those peculiar and, perhaps, excellent gifts, although I certainly must say that I cannot obey the apostle's injunction in coveting very earnestly such gifts as these.

In contrast, if some man is asked to pray who has never prayed before in public, suppose he rises and says, "O Lord, I feel myself such a sinner that I can scarcely speak to You. Lord, help me pray! O Lord, save my poor soul! Oh, that You would save my old friends! Lord, bless our minister! Be pleased to give us a revival. O Lord, I can say no more. Hear me for Jesus' sake! Amen." Well, then, you feel somehow as if you had begun to pray yourself. You feel an interest in that man, partly from fear that he might stop, and also because you are sure that what he said he meant. And if after that another should pray in the same spirit, you go out and say, "This is real prayer." I prefer three minutes of prayer like that to thirty minutes of the other sort, because the one is praying and the other is attempting to preach. Allow me to quote the advice of an old preacher concerning prayer: "Remember, the Lord will not hear you because of the *arithmetic* of your prayers, counting their numbers. He will not hear you because of the *rhetoric* of your prayers, caring for the eloquent language in which they are conveyed. He will not listen because of the *geometry* of your prayers, computing them by their length or breadth. He will not regard you because of the *music* of your prayers, caring for sweet voices or for harmony. Neither will He look at you because of the *logic* of your prayers, because they are well arranged and excellently divided. But He will hear you, and He will measure the amount of the blessings He will give you, according to the *divinity* of your prayers. If you can plead the person of Christ, and if the Holy Ghost inspires you with zeal and earnestness, the blessings that you shall ask, shall surely come to you."

I would like to burn the whole stock of old prayers and spiritual words and all those other quotations that we have been manufacturing and dislocating and repeating from man to man. I would that we came to speak to God just out of our hearts. It would be a grand thing for our prayer meetings. They would be better attended and more fruitful if every man would shake off that habit of formality and talk to God as a child talks to his father, asking Him for what we want and then sitting down and being done. I say this with all Christian earnestness. Often, because I have not chosen to pray in conventional form, people have said, "That man is not reverent." But they are not a judge of my reverence. To my own Master, I stand or fall. I do not think that Job quoted anyone. I do not think that Jacob quoted his saintly old grandfather, Abraham. I do not find Jesus Christ quoting Scripture in prayer. They did not pray in other people's words; they prayed in their own. God does not want you to go gathering up those excellent but very musty spices of the old sanctuary. He wants the new oil just distilled from the fresh olive of your own soul. He wants spices and frankincense, not of the old chests where they have been lying until they have lost their savor. He wants fresh incense and myrrh, brought from the ophir of your own soul's experience. Look well to it that you really pray: do not learn the language of prayer but seek the spirit of prayer, and God Almighty bless you and make you more mighty in your supplications.

I want you to look into your private prayers. It may be that the hinges to your prayer doors are rusty, but they do open and shut at their appointed times. Perhaps the doors are locked and cob-webbed. Or perhaps you do not neglect prayer itself, but what a tale the walls might tell! "Oh!" the walls cry out. "We have heard you when you have been in such a rush that you could hardly spend two minutes with your God. We have heard you come and spend ten minutes and not ask for anything, at least your heart did not ask. The lips moved, but the heart was silent. We have heard you groan out your soul, but we have seen you go away distrustful, not believing your prayer was heard, quoting the promise, but not thinking God would fulfill it." Surely the walls might come to-gether and fall down upon us because we have so often insulted God with our unbelief, our hurry, and with all manner of sins. We have insulted Him even at His mercy seat, on the spot where His condescension is most fully manifested. Is it not so with you? Must we not each confess it in our turn? See to it, then, that an amend-ment be made, and God make you more mighty and more suc-cessful in your prayers than before.

Look Above

Look upward, and let us weep. O God, You have given us a mighty weapon, and we have permitted it to rust. You have given us that which is mighty as Yourself, and we have let that power lie dormant. Would it not be a crime if a man were given an eye that he would not open or a hand that he would not lift up? And what must we say of ourselves when God has given us power in prayer—matchless power, full of blessedness to ourselves, and of unnumbered mercies to others—and yet that power lies still. Oh, if the universe was as still as we are, where should we be? O God, You give light to the sun, and it shines with it. You give light even to the stars, and they twinkle. To the winds You give force, and they blow. And to the air You give life, and it moves, and men breathe it in. But to Your people You have given a gift that is better than force and life and light, and yet we permit it to lie still. We almost forget that we wield the power, seldom exercising it, though it would be blessed to countless myriads. Weep, believer. We have been defeated and our banners trail in the dust because we have not prayed. Go back to your God and confess before Him that you were armed and carried bows but turned your back in the day of battle. Go to your God and tell Him that if souls are not saved, it is not because He has not power to save but because you have never travailed for perishing sinners. Your spirit has not been moved. Wake up, wake up, and be astonished: you have neglected prayer. Wrestle and strive with your God, and the blessing shall come—the early and the latter rain of His mercy, and the earth shall bring forth plenteously, and all the nations shall call Him blessed. Look up, then, and weep.

Once more, look up and rejoice. Though you have sinned against Him, He loves you still. You have not sought His face, but behold He cries to you still: "Seek my face." He does not say, "Seek me in vain." You may not have gone to the fountain, but the fountain flows as freely as before. You have shut your eye to that sun, but the sun still shines upon you with all its luster. You have not drawn near to God, but God waits to be gracious still and is ready to hear all your petitions. Behold, He says to you, "Inquire of Me concerning things to come; and concerning my sons and daughters, command me." What a blessed thing it is that the Master in heaven is always ready to hear! There is always an open ear if you have an open mouth. There is always a ready hand if you have a ready heart. You have but to cry and the Lord hears; nay, before you call, He will answer, and while you are speaking, He will hear. Go to Him at any time and wherever you are, lifting up your heart silently. And whatever your petition or request may be, ask it in Jesus' name, and it shall be done unto you.

Yet, again, look up, and change your prayers from this time forth. Look on prayer no longer as a romantic fiction or as a tedious duty. Look at it as a real power, as a real pleasure. I believe there have been many great engineers who have designed and constructed some of the most wonderful of human works, not because they would be compensated, but simply from a love of showing their own power to accomplish wonders. And shall the great Engineer attempt great works and display His power, giving you a mightier power than ever was wielded by any man apart from his God, and will you let that be still? Rather, think of some great object and strain the muscles of your supplication for it. Let every vein of your heart be full to the brim with the rich blood of desire, and struggle and wrestle and strive with God for it, using the promises and pleading the attributes of God, and see if God does not give you your heart's desire. I challenge you to exceed in prayer the Master's bounty. I throw down the gauntlet to you. Believe Him to be more than He is. Open your mouth so wide that He cannot fill it. Go to Him now for more faith than the promise warrants. Venture it, risk it, outdo the Eternal if it is possible. Or to put it simply, take your petition and needs and see if He does not honor you. See if through believing Him, He does not fulfill the promise and richly bless you with the anointing oil of His Spirit by which you will be strong in prayer. He will hear you, and you shall yet pray as prevailing princes. And one day you shall stand as more than a conqueror before the starry throne of Him who ever reigns as God over all, blessed forevermore.

*O*h, *for a mighty cry! A prevailing cry! A heaven-shaking cry! A cry that would make the gates of heaven open! A cry that God's arm could not resist! A cry of saints knit together in love and filled with holy passion! May theirs be the great plea of the atoning sacrifice, making this the burden of their cry, "O LORD, revive thy work in the midst of the years . . . in wrath remember mercy" (Hab. 3:2). Let God but throw the stone into the stagnant pool of His church, and I can see the waves of revival going out all around the world. God's kingdom will spread, and days of refreshing will come from the presence of the Lord. Let us now say in His sight that even if He does not please to hear us at the beginning of the supplication, it is our desire to wait upon Him until He does. You still remain hidden behind the mountains, yet we wait for You as they that wait for the morning. But tarry not, O our God! Make haste our Beloved.*

Chapter Five

Prayer That Is Quickly Answered

At the beginning of thy supplications the commandment came forth, and I am come to show thee; for thou art greatly beloved— Daniel 9:23.

PRAYER IS USEFUL in a thousand ways. It is spiritually what the old physicians sought after naturally — namely, a remedy of universal application. There is no need, distress, or dilemma in our lives in which prayer will not be found to be a very present help. In the case before us, Daniel had been studying the book of Jeremiah and had learned that God would accomplish seventy weeks in the desolation of Jerusalem (Dan. 9:20). But Daniel felt that there was still more to be learned, and he set his face to learn it. Daniel's mind was noble and acute, and with all its energies, Daniel sought to pry into the prophetic meaning. But rather than rely upon his own judgment, Daniel immediately devoted himself to prayer—that great key that opens mysteries.

To whom should we go for an explanation if we cannot understand a writing but to the author of the book? Daniel appealed at once to the Great Author, in whose hand Jeremiah had been the pen. In lonely retirement, the man of God knelt upon his knees and cried unto God that He would open to him the mystery of the prophecy—that he might know the full meaning of the seventy weeks, what it was that God intended to do at the end thereof, and how He would have His people behave themselves to obtain deliverance from their captivity.

Daniel asked the Lord to unloose the seals and open the volume of the book, and he was heard and favored with the knowledge that he might have sought for in vain by any other means. Luther used to say that some of his best understandings of Holy Scripture were not so much the result of meditation as they were of prayer. All students of the Word will tell you that when the hammers of learning and biblical exegesis have failed to break open a flinty text, oftentimes prayer has done it, and nuggets of gold have been found concealed therein. To every student of the Word of God who would become a well-instructed scribe, we pass along this wise saying: with all your searchings of the commentaries, with all your diggings into the original texts, with all your research among biblical scholars, *mingle much fervent prayer*. Rest assured that the old maxim, "To have prayed well is to have studied well," is worthy to be written not only upon the walls of our schools but also upon the tablets of our hearts. If you will place the Book of inspiration before your attentive eye and ask the Lord to open its meaning, the exercise of prayer itself shall be blessed by God to put your soul in the best position in which to get at the hidden meaning that lies concealed from the eye of the worldly wise. It is remarkable what is clearly manifested to meek and lowly souls when they reverently seek the guidance of their heavenly Father.

The particular point in the text to which I direct your attention is that Daniel's prayer is answered *at once*, while he is yet speaking. It is not always so. Prayer sometimes waits like a petitioner at the gate until the king comes forth to provide the blessings that the petitioner seeks. The Lord—even when He has given someone great faith—has been known to try the prayers by long delayings. He has allowed his servants' voices to echo in their ears as from a brazen sky. His servants have knocked at the golden gate, but the gate has remained immovable, as though it were rusted upon its hinges. Like Jeremiah, the servants have cried, "Thou hast covered thyself with a cloud, that our prayer should not pass through" (Lam. 3:44). Thus have true saints continued in patient waiting for months—even years—without a reply, not because they were not passionate or were not accepted, but because it pleased Him who is a sovereign and who gives according to His own pleasure. If it pleases Him to tell our patience to exercise itself, shall He not do as He wills with His own? Beggars must not be choosers either as to time, place, or form.

We must not interpret delays in prayer for denial. God's long-dated bills will be punctually honored. We must not allow Satan to shake our confidence in the God of truth by pointing to our unanswered prayers. We are dealing with One whose years are without end, to whom one day is as a thousand years. Far be it from us to count Him slack by measuring His doings by the standard of our little hour. Unanswered petitions are not unheard. God keeps a file for our prayers, which are not blown away by the wind but are treasured in the King's archives. There is a registry in the court of heaven wherein every prayer is recorded. O tried believer, your sighs and tears are not fruitless. God has a tear bottle in which the costly drops of sacred grief are put away and a book in which your holy groanings are numbered. By and by your suit shall prevail. Can you not be content to wait a little? Will not your Lord's time be better than your time? By and by He will appear to your soul's joy, causing you to put away your sackcloth and ashes of long waiting and placing on you the scarlet and fine linen of full fruition.

In the case of Daniel, however, the man greatly beloved, there was no waiting at all. In Daniel's case, the promise was true: "Before they call, I will answer; and while they are yet speaking, I will hear" (Isa. 65:24). Gabriel was called upon to fly very swiftly, as though even the flight of an angel was hardly swift enough for God's mercy. How fast the mercy of God travels, and how long His anger lingers! "Fly," said He, "bright spirit, and use your utmost power of wing! Descend to my waiting servant and fulfill his desire." My heart's desires and earnest longings are that at the beginning of our supplication we may have an answer from the throne. It is always a very blessed encouragement, a stimulus to more intense ardor, an argument for greater confidence in God, if we are favored with Daniel to receive gracious answers to our supplications at their very commencement.

Considering such a mercy from God, two points require our utmost attention. First, *there are reasons for expecting so early a bless-*

ing, and second, *there are forms in which we earnestly desire and hopefully expect it.*

Why God Answers Prayers Quickly

God will hear His people at the beginning of their prayers if the condition of their heart is ready for it. The nature of such readiness may be gathered by comparison to Daniel's heart. Our first observation is that Daniel was *determined to obtain the blessing that he was seeking.* Note carefully the expression that he used: "I set my face unto the Lord God, to seek by prayer and supplications" (Dan. 9:3). That setting of the face is expressive of resolute purpose, firm determination, undivided attention, fixed resolute perseverance: "I set my face unto the Lord." We never do anything in this world until we set our faces thoroughly toward the Lord. The warriors who win battles are those who are resolved to conquer or die. The heroes who emancipate nations are those who count no hazards and reckon no odds but are resolved that the yoke shall be broken from the neck of their country. The merchants who prosper in this world are those who do their business with all their hearts and watch for wealth with eagerness. The half-hearted man gets nowhere in the race of life, is usually considered contemptible by others, and is a misery to himself. If a thing is worth doing, it is worth doing well, and if it is not worth doing thoroughly, wise men let it alone.

This is especially true in the spiritual life. Wonders are not done for God and for the truth by sleeping men. Souls are not saved by men who hardly know or care whether they are saved themselves. Errors are not dashed from their pedestals by those who are careless concerning truth and count it of little value. Reformations have not been wrought in this world by men of lukewarm spirit and compromising policy. One fiery Luther is of more value than twenty like the half-hearted Erasmus who knew infinitely more than he felt and perhaps felt more than he dared to express. If a man would do anything for God, for the truth, for the cross of Christ, he must set his face and the whole resolve of his will to serve his God. The soldier of Christ must set his face like a flint against all opposition, and at the same moment he must set his face toward the Lord with the attentive eye of the handmaiden looking toward her mistress. If called to suffer for the truth, we must set our face toward this conflict as Jesus set his face toward Jerusalem. He who would conquer in this glorious war and overcome at the Lord's mercy seat must be resolved with his whole soul—resolved after mature thought, resolved for reasons too weighty for him to escape, resolved that from the throne of grace he will not depart without the blessing.

Never, never shall a man be unsuccessful in prayer who sets his face to win the promised mercy. If you are seeking what you ought to seek for and are seeking it through Christ and by faith in Him, the one qualification to success that we recommend is that you set your face toward the attaining of it. If there are only a dozen members in my church who have set their faces for a revival, we shall surely have it—of this my heart has no doubt. If there are only a half a dozen—like Gideon's men who lapped—who are unwavering and will not be deterred by difficulties or turned back by disappointments, as sure as God is God, He will hear the prayers of such. Even if it came down to but two or three, the promise is to two of us who are agreed as touching one thing concerning the kingdom (Matt. 18:19). And if two cannot be found but one faithful saint is left—provided that he is endowed with the spirit and ardor of Daniel—he would yet prevail as Daniel did of old. We must not fail in the setting of our face toward the Lord. I humbly but devoutly ask God the Holy Ghost to give you a solemn resolution that in the work in which you are engaged for God, you will not be satisfied unless the largest answers be vouchsafed. This was the first proof that God might safely give Daniel the blessing at once, for the prophet's heart was fixed in immutable resolve, and there was no turning him from the point. Our heavenly Father will deal with us in the same manner.

Daniel *felt deeply the misery of the people for whom he pleaded*. Read that expression, "under the whole heaven hath not been done as hath been done upon Jerusalem" (Dan. 9:12). The condition of that city—lying in ruins, her inhabitants captives, her choicest sons banished to the ends of the earth—afflicted Daniel sorely. His was not a superficial acquaintance with the sorrows of his people, but his inmost heart was embittered with the wormwood and the gall of their cup. If God intends to give us souls, He will prepare us for the honor by causing us to feel the deep ruin of our fellow creatures and the fearful doom that ruin will involve unless they shall escape from it. I would have you school yourself till you obtain a horror of the sinner's sin—surely not so strange a task if you remember your own former estate and present tendencies! How fiery was that oven through which your spirit passed when the hand of God was heavy upon you both day and night!

I want you to get a clear view of the wrath of God that threatens your own children, friends, neighbors, and kinsfolk unless they are saved. If you could get into your heart as well as into your creed the sincere belief that "the wicked shall be turned into hell, and all the nations that forget God" (Ps. 9:17), if you could recollect that for anyone who rejects Christ there remains nothing but "a certain fearful looking for of judgment and fiery indignation" (Heb. 10:27), if your soul could be made to melt for heaviness because of the woes of lost spirits—past all recall, beyond all hope or all dream of alleviation—surely you would become awfully earnest about souls. We should hear praying of a mighty sort if believers sympathized with men in their ruin. Then the soul pouring out itself in groanings that cannot be uttered would be but an ordinary thing. Then shall we prevail with God through the precious blood of Jesus when we feel intensely the sinner's need.

Daniel was ready to receive the blessing because *he felt deeply his own unworthiness of it.* I do not know that even the fifty-first Psalm is more penitential than the ninth chapter of Daniel. How the prophet confesses the people's sin and styles it by three, four, five, or more descriptive epithets—all expressive of his deep sense of its blackness. Read the chapter and note how Daniel humbly acknowledges sins of commission, sins of omission, and especially sins against the warnings of God's Word and the entreaties of God's servants. The prophet is very explicit. He lays bare his heart before the Lord, tearing off every layer from the corruption of the people. He exposes the wound to the inspection of the Great Surgeon and asks Him to heal it. I believe that the Lord is about to bless the man who personally is given a deep sense of sin, and certainly the church that is willing to make confession of its own sinfulness and unworthiness is on the eve of a visitation of love.

Let us go, then, to our God, making confession of our sins. Individual confession is needed. I have sins that you might not discover in me, but they are there. You, too, have sins in your families, in your businesses, in your private and public lives. Every man has a point of sin wherein he is separated from his fellows, and each man must therefore make his own confession—with the fullest honesty and the deepest humiliation. Each one must add to his acknowledgements the humble prayer, "Search me, O God, and know my heart: try me, and know my thoughts" (Ps. 139:23).

Are you conscious of your own personal iniquity toward the Lord your God? Then let not this day pass before a full confession has been made. And should there remain in our church any transgression unconfessed, I hope the Lord may lead us to confess it. If we have been proud, if we have been exalted by success, if there is any bickering among us, if any Christian has ill feelings toward another, let not this day end till all such evil is removed. I am very conscious that much sin may remain undetected. Oh, for great searchings of heart!

It is possible to spoil the hopes and cause God's people to miss the blessing unless every evil thing is put away. Let this be a day for purging out the old leaven, that we may keep the feast not with the leaven of malice but in holiness as becomes the disciples of Jesus (1 Cor. 5:7–8). The idols must be utterly abolished before we can expect to receive a blessing from the Lord our God. "O come, let us worship and bow down: let us kneel before the LORD our maker" (Ps. 95:6). Let us bless His name for His exceeding great goodness to us and sing of all His lovingkindness that He has shown to us. Let us confess our unworthiness, our coldness, our deadness, our lethargy, our wanderings of heart, and then, having confessed our faults, we may expect that at the very commencement God will visit us. When the vessel is empty, heaven's fountain will fill it. When the ground is dried and chapped and begins to open her mouth with thirst, down shall come the rain to gladden the soil. When we feel a sense of need, deep and crushing, then will a blessing shine forth from the presence of the Most High. "At the beginning of thy supplications the commandment came forth."

Yet, we have not exhausted the points in Daniel that deserve our imitation. You will notice that Daniel had *a clear conviction of God's power to help his people* in their distress. Daniel had the lively sense of divine power being based upon what God had done in the past. It is interesting to note in the history of the Jews how in every dark and stormy hour, their minds reverted to one particular point of their history! With a sparkle in his eyes and every muscle growing strong at the thought of the heroic day, the Israelite always thought back to the Red Sea and what the Lord did to Egypt when He divided the waters that His people might pass through. Daniel in the prayer says, "Our God . . . hast brought thy people forth out of the land of Egypt with a mighty hand, and hast gotten thee renown, as at this day" (Dan. 9:15). He lays hold upon that deep of ancient prowess and pleads after this fashion: "You can do it again, O God, and glorify Your name anew, sending deliverance to Your people."

You and I may at this moment draw comfort from the fact that this God who divided the Red Sea is our God forever and ever. He is at this hour as mighty as when He overthrew the horse and rider in the mighty waters. We worship the God who loves His chosen now even as He did of old. It is written, "But made his own people to go forth like sheep" (Ps. 78:52), and so He leads us. He led them through the wilderness and brought them to the promised rest, and so He will bring us to our eternal home. Though doubts and fears roll before us like a sea, remove them we beseech You, O God! Though our iniquities clamor behind us, swallow them up in the Red Sea of Jesus' blood! Though we march through the wilderness, yet give us heaven's manna and let the rock distill with living streams! Though we do not deserve to be visited by Your love, yet are we not Your people and the sheep of Your pasture? Are we not called by Your name? Have You not bought us with Your blood? Bring us into the promised land! Give us the heritage of Your people and bless us with the blessings of Your chosen. If we recall God's past mercies to the church and to ourselves personally, we shall be ready to receive present mercy.

The most apparent point about Daniel's prayer is Daniel's *peculiar earnestness*. To multiply expressions such as "O Lord! O Lord! O Lord!" may not always be appropriate. Such repetitions may even amount to taking God's name in vain. But it is not so with Daniel. His repetitions are forced from the depths of his soul, "O Lord, hear; O Lord, forgive; O Lord, hearken and do!" (Dan. 9:19). These are the fiery volcanic eruptions of a soul on fire, heaving terribly. Jesus Himself, when He prayed most passionately, prayed three times, using the same words. Variety of expression sometimes shows that the mind is not altogether absorbed in the object but is still able to consider the fashioning of words for its utterance. But when the heart becomes entirely consumed in the desire, it cannot stay to polish and fashion its words. It seizes upon any expressions nearest to hand, and with these it continues its entreaties. As long as God understands it, the troubled mind has no concern about its modes of speech. Daniel here, with what the old divines would have called multiplied ingeminations, groans himself upward till he gains the summit of his desires.

To what shall I liken the pleadings of the man greatly beloved? It seems to me as though he thundered and lightninged at the gate of heaven. He stood there before God and said to Him, "O thou Most High, You have brought me to this place as You brought Jacob to the Jabbok, and with You all night I mean to stay and wrestle till the break of day. I cannot and will not let You go unless You bless me." No prayer is at all likely to bring down an immediate answer if it is not a fervent prayer. "The effectual fervent prayer of a righteous man availeth much" (James 5:16), but if it is not fervent, we cannot expect to find it effectual or prevalent. We must get rid of the icicles that hang about our lips. We must ask the Lord to thaw the ice caves of our soul and make our hearts like a furnace of fire heated seven times hotter. If our hearts do not burn within us, we may well question whether Jesus is with us. Those who are neither cold nor hot He has threatened to spew out of His mouth (Rev. 3:16). How can we expect His favor if we fall into a condition so obnoxious to Him? "For our God is a consuming fire" (Heb. 12:29), and He will not have communion with us until our souls grow to be like consuming fires, too. Unless we are warm with love for God, we cannot expect the love of God to manifest itself in us to its highest degree.

I have seen apostolic holiness revived within our church. I will say before the throne of God that I have seen as earnest and as true a godliness as Paul or Peter ever witnessed. I have seen such godly zeal, such holiness, such devotion to the Master's business as Christ Himself would look upon with joy and satisfaction. But there are others who never enter heartily into our projects of concern or unite with our gatherings of prayer. To them I say, "My dear brethren, if you are indeed with us, if you have fellowship with us and with the Father and His Son Jesus Christ, I beseech you to ask the Lord to make you more earnest than the most earnest of us have ever been. If you have been slow either in generosity of your giving or in the earnestness of your pleading, ask the Lord that you may henceforth double your pace and do more in the time that remains for you in this life than anyone might dream possible."

By way of summary, the first reason we may expect a speedy answer to prayer is when the condition of the suppliant is as God would have it. If the whole church shall be brought to set its face, to be conscious of the deep need of sinners, to confess its own sin, to be mindful of God's mercy, and to be passionately in earnest for a blessing, I cannot for my own part see the slightest reason why at the beginning of the prayer the commandment should not go forth.

Second, I believe we have every reason to expect a blessing when we consider *the mercy itself.* That which we as a church are seeking is to see our own personal holiness deepened and revived, and we want to see sinners saved. Is that not in itself so good a thing that we may expect the Giver of every good and perfect gift to give it to us? We seek that which is for the good of His church. A brother once remarked in prayer that none of us would let our spouse ask again and again for any good thing if it were in our power to give it to her. We would feel it our greatest delight to do so. And shall the bride, the Lamb's wife, find her Husband less kind than we are to our wives? No. If Christ's church pleads with her own Husband, she cannot be refused. Depend upon it, her royal Husband will give her according to His infinite fullness.

What we ask is for God's glory. We are not seeking a gift that may glorify *us*, bringing honor to human prowess or to human wisdom. We see that which will put crowns upon the head of our gracious God, and we seek it with the one pure desire that He may be glorified. Above all, we ask that which is dear to the heart of Christ. Jesus is the friend of sinners—for sinners He lived, He died, He rose, He pleads, and He reigns in glory. If we come to God and say to Him, "By the blood and wounds of Jesus, by the griefs of Gethsemane, and by the groans of Calvary, hear us," how can it be that we shall be kept waiting? No, I gather that if this is the burden of the prayer, at the beginning we shall receive.

The third thing that encourages me is *the nature of the relations that exist between God and us.* Is not that a choice phrase—"O man greatly beloved"? You will perhaps say, "It is easy to understand that God should send so swift an answer to Daniel because Daniel was greatly beloved." Has your unbelief made you forget that *you* are greatly beloved, too? As a believer in Jesus Christ, you will not be at all presumptuous if you apply to yourself the title of "greatly beloved." Must you not have been greatly beloved to have been bought with the precious blood of Christ, as of a lamb without blemish and without spot? When God spared not His own Son but gave Him up for you, must you not have been greatly beloved? You were called by grace, led to a Savior, and made a child of God and an heir of heaven. That proves, does it not, a very great and superabounding love? That time, whether your path has been rough with troubles or smooth with goodness, I have no doubt it has been full of proofs that you are greatly beloved.

When I look back upon my own life, I must confess my unworthiness and acknowledge my sin most sincerely, and yet I dare to feel and to say that I am a man greatly beloved of my God. He has given me such distinguished mercies to enjoy, when I have served not even the least of them, that I cannot help saying, "Who crowneth thee with lovingkindness and tender mercies" (Ps. 103:4). I make my boast in the tender mercy of my God all the more freely because I am sure that you are also specially beloved of heaven. The more unworthy you feel yourself to be, the more evidence you have that nothing but unspeakable love could have led the Lord Jesus to save such a soul as yours. The more unworthiness the saint feels, the more proof of the great love of God in having chosen him and called him and made him an heir of bliss.

If there is such love between God and us, let us pray very boldly. Do not let us go to God as though we were strangers or as though He were unwilling to give—we are greatly beloved. "He that spared not his own Son, but delivered him up for us all, how shall he not with him also freely give us all things" (Rom. 8:32). Come boldly, for despite the whispering of Satan and the doubtings of your own heart, you are greatly beloved. Jesus said, "If ye shall ask any thing in my name, I will do it" (John 14:14). Who will refuse to ask when such encouragements are suggested to our minds?

How God Answers Prayer

Could I have my heart's desire, I would crave a blessing *for every reader.* I wish the blessing would come upon every pastor that they might preach with more power and pray with more fervor and that their spiritual life might be healthier and more vigorous. I wish the blessing might come on those involved in the management and leadership of the church, since they need much more grace upon them than falls to the lot of ordinary men. I pray that you may be made examples to your flock. I wish that the Holy Spirit may fall on all of you workers for Christ. The Lord bless you Sunday school teachers. May you weep in your classes! May you pray for your children before you begin to talk with them! May those of you who teach classes of men and women have a rich blessing! How would it be if this very day you felt the first waves of a great revival. I wish the Lord's power would come upon some of His people who do nothing—that they may be dreadfully miserable and so unhappy that they cannot stay at home but are compelled to start out and do good. You who are working, may God help you to work with heart and soul—not doing it as a matter of routine but doing it with your very life—as though your heart's blood warmed in the work and your soul's breath were in every word you spoke.

It would be a very blessed song of grace if every one of us felt, "Perhaps there is something more I could do for Christ; I shall do it at once. Perhaps there is something I might give to Christ, some Christian service I can become involved in. Perhaps God has given me a talent that I have never used or I have treated like an old sword that hangs up unfurbished. Now, before the Lord, I lift my hand to heaven, and I ask that if I have anything—even though it is the smallest talent—I have not used, He will help me to use it at once."

We live in such a dark world that we must not waste the tiniest piece of candle. The night is so dark that even a glowworm must not refuse to give its feeble ray. Each of us must give personal service to Christ. Do you not know that all God's people are priests? God's priests are those who are alive from the dead by the power of the Holy Spirit, and every man and woman who loves

Jesus is a priest to God. Let us never say, "We have a minister; let him serve God for us." I can do nothing to carry the responsibilities God has given you. Serve God yourself. It is as much as I can do to serve Him, and it is only by His grace that I am upheld under my own load. But as for being a proxy for you, I cannot do anything of the kind. Personally, you were bought with blood; personally, you hope to enter heaven; personally, then, consecrate yourself to the Lord, and if you so do, oh, what a blessing it will be! May God send a new and quickened life in His people at the commencement of our supplication.

How early and sweet a blessing it is when the Lord gives us some *conversions*. Whom shall we especially plead for? What kind of conversions do we desire? What a blessing if the Lord would call by grace some of the children of the church members! Oh, for salvation for our sons and daughters! Pray for them, parents, pray for them. Pray now, and the Lord will hear you. Or suppose He were to give to some dear brother the soul of his wife for whom he has prayed so long. I would take it as a special favor if the Lord would give us our dearest friends. Perhaps God will deliver you from some darling sin you cannot give up and that will be your everlasting ruin. I remember M'Cheyne says, "Christ gives last knocks." That is a very sorrowful thought. He knocks at the door, but there is such a thing as a last knock, and there are those who will get their last knock before long. He will never knock again. May God give us their souls this day!

Oh, for a mighty cry! A prevailing cry! A heaven-shaking cry! A cry that would make the gates of heaven open! A cry that God's arm could not resist! A cry of saints knit together in love and filled with holy passion! May theirs be the great plea of the atoning sacrifice, making this the burden of their cry, "O LORD, revive thy work in the midst of the years . . . in wrath remember mercy" (Hab. 3:2). Let God but throw the stone into the stagnant pool of His church, and I can see the waves of revival going out all around the world. God's kingdom will spread, and days of refreshing will come from the presence of the Lord. Let us now say in His sight that even if He does not please to hear us at the beginning of the supplication, it is our desire to wait upon Him until He does. You still remain hidden behind the mountains, yet we wait for You as they that wait for the morning. But tarry not, O our God! Make haste our Beloved.

Some people's prayers have no work in them. Prayer that prevails with God is a real workingman's prayer. It is prayer where the petitioner, like a Samson, shakes the gates of mercy and labors to pull them up rather than be denied an entrance. We do not want fingertip prayers that barely touch the burden. We need shoulder prayers that bear a load of earnestness and are not to be denied their desire. We do not want those dainty runaway knocks at the door of mercy that some give when they perform for others at prayer meetings. We ask for the knocking of a man who means to stop at mercy's gate till it opens and all his need shall be supplied. The energetic, vehement violence of the man who is not to be denied but intends to carry heaven by storm until he wins his heart's desire—this is the prayer that ministers covet of their people.

Chapter Six

The Power of Prayer and the Pleasure of Praise

Ye also helping together by prayer for us, that for the gift bestowed upon us by the means of many persons thanks may be given by many on our behalf. For our rejoicing is this, the testimony of our conscience, that in simplicity and godly sincerity, not with fleshly wisdom, but by the grace of God, we have had our conversation in the world, and more abundantly to you-ward—2 Corinthians 1:11–12.

THE APOSTLE PAUL'S LIFE was in constant danger, and it was only through singular providences that he had been delivered from imminent peril in Asia. During the great riot at Ephesus, Demetrius and his fellow shrine makers raised a fierce tumult against Paul when they realized that their craft was in danger (Acts 19:24–27). Paul's life was so greatly in jeopardy that he writes, "We were pressed out of measure, above strength, insomuch that we despaired even of life" (2 Cor. 1:8). The apostle attributes to God alone the preservation of his life. And if Paul referred also to the occasion at Lystra when he was stoned and left for dead (Acts 14:19), there is much appropriateness in his blessing, "God which raiseth the dead" (2 Cor. 1:9).

Paul, moreover, argues from the fact that the God who had thus delivered him in the past was still his helper in the present and that He would be with him also in the future (2 Cor. 1:10). Paul was a master accountant whose faith was always computing by the believer's *Rule of Three*—he argues from the past to the present and from the present to things yet to come. Note in this verse that precedes our text a brilliant example of the powerful conclusion Paul derives by the *Rule of Three*—"Who delivered us from so great a death, and doth deliver: in whom we trust that he will yet deliver us." Because our God is "the same yesterday, and today, and for ever" (Heb. 13:8), His love in times past is an infallible assurance of His kindness today, and an equally certain pledge of His faithfulness in the future. Whatever our circumstances are, however perplexing our pathway may be, and however dark our horizon, if we argue by the rule of *He has, He does, He will,* our comfort can never be destroyed. Courage, then, to you who are afflicted. If you had a changeable God to deal with, your souls might be full of bitterness; but because He is unchanging, every repeated manifestation of His grace should make it easier for you to rest in Him. Every renewed experience of His faithfulness should confirm your confidence in His grace. May the most blessed Spirit teach you to grow in holy confidence in our ever faithful Lord.

Although Paul acknowledged God's hand alone in his deliverance, he was not so foolish as to deny or undervalue the secondary causes. On the contrary, having first praised the God of all comfort, the text shows how he remembers with gratitude the earnest prayers of many loving intercessors. Gratitude to God must never become an excuse for ingratitude to man. It is true that Jehovah shielded the apostle to the Gentiles, but He did it in answer to prayer. The chosen vessel was not broken by the rod of the wicked, for the outstretched hand of the God of heaven was his defense; but God's hand was outstretched because the people of Corinth and the saints of God everywhere had prevailed at the throne of grace by their united supplications. With gratitude, those successful pleadings are mentioned: "Ye also helping together by prayer for us." And Paul desires the Corinthians to unite their praises with his "that for the gift bestowed upon us by the means of many persons thanks may be given by many on our behalf," for he adds that he has a claim upon their love through the simple and sincere preaching of the Word to them.

May the anointing Spirit descend upon the words of the text and make them profitable to us. We shall, first, *acknowledge the power of united prayer*. Second, we shall note Paul's *valuing of united praise*. Third, we shall examine *a claim that belongs to all ministers of God who sincerely labor for souls*.

The Power of United Prayer

It has pleased God to make prayer the abounding and rejoicing river through which most of our precious mercies flow to us. It is the golden key that unlocks the abundant granaries of our heavenly Joseph. It is written upon each of the mercies of the covenant, "I will yet for this be inquired of by the house of Israel, to do it for them" (Ez. 36:37). While some of God's mercies come to men unsought, there are other mercies that are bestowed only upon those who ask and therefore receive, who seek and therefore find, who knock and therefore gain an entrance.

Why has God been pleased to command us to pray at all? It really is not difficult to discover the answer, for prayer *glorifies God* by positioning man in the humblest posture of worship. The creature in prayer acknowledges His Creator with reverence and confesses Him to be the giver of every good and perfect gift. The believer's eye is lifted up to behold the glory of the Lord while his knee is bent to the earth in the lowliness of acknowledged weakness. Though prayer is not the highest form of adoration—or otherwise it would be continued by the saints in heaven—it is the most humble and the most fitting to set forth the glory of the perfect One as He is beheld by imperfect flesh and blood. From our claim of relationship with "Our Father" in the Lord's prayer right on to our ascribing the only true God with "the kingdom, and the power, and the glory," every sentence of prayer honors the Most High (Matt. 6:9–13). The groans and tears of humble petitioners are as truly acceptable as the continual "Holy, holy, holy" of the cherubim and seraphim (Rev. 4:8), for in their very essence, all truthful confessions of personal fault are but a homage paid to the infinite perfections of the Lord of hosts. The Lord is more honored by our prayers than by the unceasing smoke of the holy incense of the altar that stood before the veil.

Moreover, the act of prayer *teaches us our unworthiness*, which is no small blessing to such proud beings as we. If God gave us mercies without constraining us to pray for them, we should never know how poor we are. A true prayer is an inventory of needs, a catalog of necessities, an exposure of secret wounds, a revelation of hidden poverty. While it is an application to divine wealth, it is also a confession of human emptiness. I believe that the most healthy state of a Christian is to be always empty and always depending upon the Lord for supplies. It is to be always poor in self and rich in Jesus. It is to know our personal weaknesses and yet be mighty through God to do great exploits. While prayer adores God, it lays the creature where he should be—in the very dust.

Prayer is in itself—apart from the answer that it brings—a great benefit to the Christian. As the runner gains strength for the race by daily exercise, so for the great race of life do we acquire energy by the hallowed labor of prayer. Prayer plumes the wings of God's young eaglets so that they may learn to mount above the clouds. Prayer brings inner strength to God's warriors and sends them forth to spiritual battle with their muscles firm and their armor in place. As the sun arises from the chambers of the east, an earnest saint comes out of his prayer closet rejoicing like a strong man to run his race. Prayer is that uplifted hand of Moses that routs the Amalekites more than the sword of Joshua. It is the arrow shot from the chamber of the prophet foreboding defeat to the Syrians. What if I say that prayer clothes the believer with the attributes of Deity, infuses human weakness with divine strength, turns human folly into heavenly wisdom, and gives to troubled mortals the serenity of the immortal God. I know not what prayer cannot do! I thank You, great God, for the mercy seat—a wonderful gift of Your marvelous lovingkindness. Help us to use it correctly!

As many mercies are transported from heaven in the ship of prayer, so *there are many special mercies that can only be brought to us by the fleets of united prayer*. Many are the good things that God will give to his lonely Elijahs and Daniels, but if two of you agree as touching anything that you ask, there is no limit to God's bountiful answers (Matt. 18:19). Peter might never have been brought out of prison had it not been that prayer was made without ceasing by *all* the church for him (Acts 12:5). Pentecost might never have come had not *all* the disciples been "with one accord in one place" (Acts 2:1), waiting for the descent of the tongues of fire. God is pleased to answer individual prayers, but at times He seems to say, "You may entreat My favor, but I will not see your face unless your brethren are with you." Why is this? I take it that our gracious Lord is setting forth His own esteem for the communion of saints. "I believe in the communion of saints" is one article of the great Christian creed, but how few saints understand it. And yet there is such a thing as real union among God's people.

We cannot afford to lose the help and love of our brethren. Augustine says, "The poor are made for the rich, and the rich are made for the poor." I do not doubt but that strong saints are made for weak saints and that the weak saints bring special benedictions upon mature believers. There is a completeness in the whole body of Christ—each joint owes something to every other joint, and the whole body is bound together by that which every joint supplies. There are certain glands in the human body whose distinct value the anatomist hardly understands. Yet, if a particular gland is removed, the whole body may suffer to a high degree. Similarly, there may be some believers of whom we say, "I cannot tell what good that Christian does." Yet, were that insignificant and apparently useless member removed, the whole body might be made to suffer. This is probably why so many weighty gifts of heaven's love are granted only to combined petitioning—that we may perceive the value of the whole body and so may be compelled to recognize the vital union that divine grace has made and daily maintains among the people of God.

Is it not a happy thought that the very poorest and most obscure member can add something to the church's strength? We cannot all preach or provide leadership or even give gold and silver, but we can all contribute our prayers. There is no convert—even the newest believer reborn in grace—who cannot pray. Every believer in Jesus can pray. Sickness, age, obscurity, illiteracy, and poverty cannot hinder the power of prayer. This is the church's riches. There is a spiritual chest within the church into which we should all drop our loving intercessions as into the treasury of the Lord. Even the widow—without her two pennies—can give her offering to this treasury. The value placed upon union and communion among the people of God is seen by the fact that there are certain mercies that are bestowed only when the saints pray unitedly. How we ought to feel this bond of union! How we ought to pray for one another! How, as often as the church meets together for supplication, should we all make it our duty to be there! How much might we be robbing ourselves by failing to heed the command: "Not forsaking the assembling of ourselves together, as the manner of some is" (Heb. 10:25).

The prayer meeting is an invaluable institution ministering strength to all other meetings and agencies. This brings a further observation. *This united prayer should specially be made for the ministers of God.* It is for them in particular that this public prayer is intended. Paul asks for it: "Brethren, pray for us" (1 Thess. 5:25). God's ministers will always confess that this is the secret source of their strength. The prayers of the people must be the might of the ministers. Keep in mind why the minister more than any other person in the church needs the earnest prayers of the people. Is not *his position the most perilous?* Satan knows if he can once smite through the minister's heart, there will be a general confusion among God's people. It is around the standard bearer that the fight is thickest. There the battle-axes ring upon the helmets and the arrows are bent upon the armor, for the foe knows that if he can cut down the standard, he will strike a heavy blow and cause deep discouragement. Press around your minister, then, you men at arms! Knights of the red cross rally to his defense, for the fight grows hot. The person you call to the office of the ministry needs you to stand fast at his side in his hourly conflicts. The life of a minister is so perilous that I may well cry, "All hands on deck!" Let every saint give himself to prayer; let even the weakest saint become instant in supplication.

The minister, standing in such a perilous position, has *a solemn weight of responsibility resting on him.* Every man should be his brother's keeper to a degree, but woe to the watchmen of God if they are not faithful. It is to the watchmen's hands that the blood of souls and the ruin of men are required if they fail to preach the gospel fully and faithfully. There are times when this burden of the Lord weighs upon God's ministers until they cry out in pain as if their hearts would burst with anguish. There will come times with every preacher of the gospel—if he is faithful to what he should be—when he will be in dread suspense for his hearers and must call upon his God for help since he is overwhelmed with the burden of men's souls. Do pray for those in the ministry. If God gives a minister to your church and you accept the gift most cheerfully, do not so despise both God and the minister as to leave the minister without your prayers.

The preservation and health of the minister *is one of the most vital points to the church.* You may lose a sailor from the ship, and that is very bad—both for him and for you—but if the captain should be washed overboard, what is the vessel to do? Therefore, though prayer is to be made for every person in the church, yet for the minister is it to be offered first and foremost because of the position that he occupies? And then, *how much more is asked of him than of you?* If you are to keep a private table for personal spiritual growth, he is, as it were, to keep a public table—a feast of good spiritual things for all comers. How shall he do this unless his Master gives him rich provisions? If you are to shine as a candle in a house, the minister is to be a lighthouse to be seen far across the deep. How shall he shine the whole night long unless he is trimmed by his Master and fresh oil is given him from heaven? The minister's influence is wider than yours: if it is for evil, he shall be a deadly upas whose spreading boughs poison all beneath his shadow. But if God makes him a star in His right hand, his ray of light shall cheer with its genial influence whole nations and whole periods of time. If there is any truth in all this, I implore you to generously and constantly pray for those who minister to you.

I find that the Greek word for *helping together* implies *very earnest work.* Some people's prayers have no work in them. Prayer that prevails with God is a real workingman's prayer. It is prayer where the petitioner, like a Samson, shakes the gates of mercy and labors to pull them up rather than be denied an entrance. We do not want fingertip prayers that barely touch the burden. We need shoulder prayers that bear a load of earnestness and are not to be denied their desire. We do not want those dainty runaway knocks at the door of mercy that some give when they perform for others at prayer meetings. We ask for the knocking of a man who means to stop at mercy's gate till it opens and all his need shall be supplied. The energetic, vehement violence of the man who is not to be denied but intends to carry heaven by storm until he wins his heart's desire—this is the prayer that ministers covet of their people. Melancthon, it is said, derived great comfort from the information that certain poor weavers—women and children—had met together to pray for the Reformation. Yes, Melancthon had solid ground for comfort. It was not Luther only, but the thousands of poor persons who sang psalms in the fields and the hundreds of serving men and women who offered supplications that made the Reformation what it was. I have told my congregation a hundred times that all the blessing that God has given us here, all the increase to our church, has been due to their earnest, fervent supplications. There have been heaven-moving seasons when we have felt we could die sooner than not be heard by God, when we carried our church on our bosom as a mother carries her child, when we felt a yearning and a travailing in birth for the souls of men. "What hath God wrought?" we may truly ask, when we see our church increasing daily and multitudes still hanging upon our lips to listen to the Word.

Shall we now cease from our prayers? Shall we now say to the Great High Priest, "It is enough"? Shall we now pluck the glowing coals from the altar and quench the burning incense? Shall we now refuse to bring the morning and evening lambs of prayer and praise to the sacrifice? O children of Ephraim, being armed and carrying bows, will you turn your backs in the day of battle? The sea is divided before you and the Jordan is driven back. Will you refuse to march through the depths? God, even your God, goes up before you. The shout of a King is heard in the midst of your hosts. Will you now be cowardly and refuse to go up and possess the land? Will you now lose your first love? Shall "Ichabod" be written upon the entrance to your church? Shall it be said that God has forsaken you? Shall the day come in which the daughters of Philistia rejoice and the sons of Syria triumph? If not, to your knees again with all the force of prayer! If not, to your vehement supplications once more! If you would not see good blighted and evil triumphant, clasp each other's hands again, and in the name of Him who ever lives to intercede, once more be prevalent in prayer that the blessing may again descend. "Ye also helping together by prayer for us."

The Value of United Praise

Praise should always follow answered prayer. The mist of earth's gratitude should rise as the sun of heaven's love warms the ground. Has the Lord been gracious to you and inclined His ear to the voice of your prayer? Then praise Him as long as you live. Deny not a song to Him who has answered your prayer and given you the desire of your heart. To be silent over God's mercies is to incur the guilt of shocking ingratitude, and ingratitude is one of the worst of crimes. I trust you will not follow the example of the nine lepers who failed to return to give thanks to their healing Lord (Luke 17:17). To forget to praise God is to refuse to benefit ourselves, for praise—like prayer—is exceedingly useful to the spiritual man. Praise is a high and healthy exercise. To dance before the Lord like David is to quicken the blood in the veins and make the pulse beat at a healthier rate (2 Sam. 6:14). Praise brings us a great feast as when David gave every man "a good piece of flesh, and a flagon of wine" (2 Sam. 6:19). Praise is the most heavenly of Christian duties. The angels may not pray, but they never cease to praise God both day and night. To bless God for mercies received is to benefit our fellow believers: "the humble shall hear thereof, and be glad" (Ps. 34:2). Others who have been in similar circumstances shall take comfort if we can say, "O magnify the LORD with me, and let us exalt his name together . . . This poor man cried, and the LORD heard him" (Ps. 34:3, 6). Tongue-tied Christians are a sad dishonor to the church. We have some whom the devil appears to have gagged, and the loudest music they ever make is when they are champing the bit of their silence. I would that in all such cases, the tongue of the dumb may sing.

As praise is good and pleasant—blessing man and glorifying God—*united praise has a very special commendation.* United praise is like music in concert. The sound of one instrument is exceedingly sweet, but when hundreds of instruments — both wind and stringed—are all combined, the orchestra sends forth a noble volume of harmony. The praise of one Christian is accepted before God like a grain of incense, but the praise of many is like a censer full of frankincense smoking up before the Lord. Combined praise is an anticipation of heaven, for in that general assembly, they altogether with one heart and voice praise the Lord.

Public praise edifies the Christian himself. How many burdens has it removed? When I hear the shout of praise among God's people, it warms my heart. When the rolling waves of majestic praise display their full force, there is no music like it to my heart. I love to hear God's people sing in a grand harmony of praise. Oh, for a sacred song, a shout of lofty praise in which every man's soul beats the time, and every man's tongue sounds the tune, and each singer feels compelled to excel his fellow in gratitude and love! There is something exceedingly delightful in the union of true hearts in the worship of God, and when these hearts are expressed in song, how sweet the charming sounds. I think we ought to have a praise meeting once a week. We have our regular prayer meetings, but why do we not have praise meetings? Surely, seasons should be set apart for services made up of praise from beginning to end.

As united prayer should be offered especially for ministers, so *united praise should often take the same aspect*. The whole church should praise and bless God for the mercy rendered to her members through its pastors. Hear how our apostle puts it again: "That for the gift bestowed upon us by the means of many persons, thanks may be given by many on our behalf." We should praise God for good ministers *that they live*, for when they die, much of their work dies with them. It is astonishing how a reformation will press on while Luther and Calvin live, and yet how quickly the reformation ceases when the reformers die. The spirits of good men are immortal only in a sense. The churches of God in this age are like the Israelites in the times of the judges: when the judges died, the people went after graven images again. And it is so now. While God spares the minister, the church prospers; but when the minister dies, the zeal that he blew to a flame smolders among the ashes. In nine cases out of ten—if not in ninety-nine out of every hundred—the prosperity of a church rests on the minister's life. God so ordains it to humble us. There should be gratitude, then, for spared life.

But there should be even greater gratitude for *preserved character*, for when a minister falls, what a disgrace it is! It is certain that there will always be some hypocrites who will take the name of a minister to get some sort of reputation. But if the faithful minister is made to hold fast his integrity, there should be constant gratitude to God for his behalf. If the minister is kept *well supplied with divine truth,* if he is like a springing well, if God gives him the ability to bring out of His treasury things both new and old to feed His people, there should be hearty thanks. And if the minister is kept *sound*—not going aside to philosophy on the one hand or to a narrowness of doctrine on the other—there should be thanksgiving. If God brings the masses to hear him, and above all, if souls are converted and saints are edified, there should be never-ceasing honor and praise to God. Perhaps this is a privilege we have come to take for granted. Yet, I have stayed in houses with godly men with whom I held sweet communion but who cannot attend what was once their place of worship. Why not? "Sir," they say, "can I go to a place of worship where the ministers deny every word of Scripture?" If God were to take away the ministers who preach the gospel boldly and plainly, you would cry to God to give you the candlestick back again. We still have among us ministers who are faithful to God and preach the whole truth as it is in Jesus. Be thankful for your ministers, I say again, for if you were placed where some believers are, you would cry out to your God, "Lord, send us back Your prophets. Send us a famine of bread or water, but do not send us a famine of the Word of God!

The Minister's Joyful Claim

"For our rejoicing in this, the testimony of our conscience, that in simplicity and godly sincerity, not with fleshly wisdom, but by the grace of God, we have had our conversation in the world, and more abundantly to you-ward." Next to the comfort of the finished salvation of God, a man's comfort must come from the testimony of his own conscience. And to a minister, what a testimony it is that he has preached the gospel in simplicity. This means preaching without double-mindedness—saying one thing and meaning another. It is to preach the gospel meaning what you say, having a single heart, desiring God's glory and the salvation of men. And what a blessing to have preached it simply—that is to say, without difficult words, without polished phrases, never straining after oratorical embellishments. How accursed must be the life of a minister who profanes the pulpit to the dignity of eloquence. How desperate his deathbed will be when he remembers that he made an exhibition of his powers of speech rather than of the solid things that make for the winning of souls. That conscience may well be easy that can speak of having dealt with God's truth in simplicity.

The apostle says also that he had preached the gospel with sincerity—that is, he had preached the truth meaning it, feeling it, preached it so that none could accuse him of being false. The Greek word for *sincerity* has something in it of sunlight, and he is the true minister of God who preaches what he would wish to have hung up in the sunlight or who has the sunlight shining right through him. I am afraid no minister is like white glass; most of us are colored a little, but happy is the minister who seeks to get rid of as much of the coloring matter as possible so that the light of the gospel may shine straight through him—as clear as it comes from the Sun of Righteousness. Paul had preached with simplicity and sincerity. And he adds, "Not with fleshly wisdom." What stories I have heard of what fleshly wisdom will do. Some reduce Scripture to a book of silly myths, others say that there are some good things in the Bible though there are a great many mistakes, and others fling the whole Bible away as to its inspiration. Sad! sad! sad! that the church has gone to such a length as that. How earnestly should we decry fleshly wisdom! I am afraid that when we hear a minister, we like his delivery to be excellent and find fault unless he shows some degree of talent. I wonder whether that is not a sin? I am half inclined to think it is. I think we should look less every day to talent and more and more to the matter of the gospel that is preached. If a minister is blessed with eloquent speech, are we more profited by him or might it be to our weakness? I sometimes wonder whether we should return to the days of fishermen and give no ministers any education whatsoever. Perhaps we should just send ministers to preach the truth simply rather than give them all sorts of learning that is of no earthly use to them but only helps them to pervert the simplicity of God. I love that word in my text—"Not with fleshly wisdom."

And now I lay my claim before my church, as my conscience bears me witness—I lay my claim to this boasting of our apostle. I have preached God's gospel in simplicity. I do not know how I can preach it more simply or honestly. I have preached it sincerely—the Searcher of all hearts knows that. And I have not preached it with fleshly wisdom, and that for one excellent reason—I have been compelled to keep to the simple testimony of the Lord by the grace of God. If any success has been achieved, it has been grace that has done it all. "And more especially to you-ward." I have warned, entreated, exhorted, pleaded, wept, prayed. To some members I have been a spiritual parent in Christ, to many I have been a teacher and an edifier in the gospel, and I hope to all I have been a sincere friend in Christ Jesus. Therefore have I claimed their prayers—*theirs* more than any other people's. Remember this phrase, "especially to you-ward," as you consider your ministers in your prayers. Do pray for them still! Is the whole congregation saved yet? Plead with God for the sake of the unconverted. Are some hard hearts unbroken? Ask God to make the hammer strike. And while there are some still unmelted, pray God to make the Word like a fire. Pray for your ministers that God may make them mighty. The church still needs more of the loud voice of God to wake it from its sleep. Ask God to bless all His sent servants. Plead with Him with divine energy that His kingdom may come and His will be done on earth as it is in heaven.

Childlike confidence makes us pray as none else can. It causes a man to pray for great things that he would never have asked for if he had not learned this confidence. It also causes him to pray for little things that many people are afraid to ask for, because they have not yet felt toward God the confidence of children. I have often felt that it requires more confidence in God to pray to Him about a little thing than about great things. We imagine that our great things are somehow worthy of God's attention, though in truth they are little enough to Him. And then we think that our little things must be so insignificant that it is an insult to bring them before Him. We need to realize that what is very important to a child may be very small to his parent, and yet the parent measures the thing not from his own point of view but from the child's. You heard your little boy the other day crying bitterly. The cause of the pain was a splinter in his finger. While you did not call in three surgeons to extract it, the splinter was a great thing to that little sufferer. Standing there with eyes all wet through tears of anguish, it never occurred to that boy that his pain was too small a thing for you to care about. What were mothers and fathers made for but to look after the small concerns of little children? And God our Father is a good father who pities us as fathers pity their children. He counts the stars and calls them all by name, yet He heals the broken in heart and binds up their wounds.

Chapter Seven

The Conditions of Power in Prayer

And whatsoever we ask, we receive of him, because we keep his commandments, and do those things that are pleasing in his sight. And this is his commandment, That we should believe on the name of his Son Jesus Christ, and love one another, as he gave us commandment. And he that keepeth his commandments dwelleth in him, and he in him. And hereby we know that he abideth in us, by the Spirit which he hath given us—1 John 3:22–24.

I HAVE OFTEN SPOKEN to my congregation on the importance of prayer, especially desiring to stir up the members to pray for me and for the Lord's work in our church. Truly, I do not think I have had a more weighty subject or one that weighs more upon my soul. If I were only allowed to offer one request from church members, it would be this: "Brethren, pray for us" (2 Thess. 3:1). Of what use can our ministry be without the divine blessing, and how can we expect the divine blessing unless it is sought for by the church of God? I would say it even with tears: "Brethren, pray for us." Do not restrain prayer. On the contrary, be abundant in intercession, for only through prayer can the prosperity of a church be increased or even maintained.

But then, the question occurs: What if there is something in the church that prevents our prayers from being successful? That is a prerequisite question that must be considered most earnestly before the church is exhorted to intercession. The Word of God is clear that the prayers of unholy people will soon become abominations to God. "And when ye spread forth your hands, I will hide mine eyes from you: yea, when ye make many prayers, I will not hear" (Isa. 1:15). Churches may fall into such a condition that their devotions will be an iniquity; "even the solemn meeting" will be a weariness to the Lord. There may be evils in the heart of any believer that may render it impossible for God, in consistency with His own character and attributes, to have any regard for our intercessions. If we regard iniquity in our hearts, the Lord will not hear us. According to the text, there are some things that the people of God must possess or their prayers will fall short of the mark. The text tells us, "Whatsoever we ask, we receive of him, because we keep his commandments, and do those things that are pleasing in his sight." We need to consider the essentials to power in prayer—what we must do, what we must be, what we must have, if we are to prevail habitually with God in prayer.

The Essentials of Power in Prayer

We must make a few distinctions at the outset. I maintain that there is a great difference between the prayer of a sinner who is seeking God's mercy and the prayer of a man who is saved. I say to every reader—whatever your character—if you sincerely seek the mercy of God through Jesus Christ, you shall have it. Whatever may have been your previous condition of life, if you penitently seek Jehovah's face through the appointed Mediator, you will find Him. If the Holy Spirit has taught you to pray, hesitate no longer, but hasten to the cross and there rest your guilty soul on Jesus. The only qualification I know of for the sinner's first prayer is sincerity.

But we must speak in a different manner to believers. The people of God are heard just as the sinner is heard and daily find the needful grace that every seeker receives in answer to prayer. Yet the child of God comes under a special discipline peculiar to the regenerated family. In that discipline, answers to prayer occupy a high position and are of a high importance. Believers are meant to enjoy many blessings over and above mere salvation. There are mercies, blessings, comforts, and favors that render the believer's present life effective, happy, and honorable, but these are not given irrespective of his character. These blessings are not the essential matters with regard to salvation that the believer possesses unconditionally, for they are covenant blessings. But we now refer to the honors and special favors of God's house that are given or withheld according to our obedience as the Lord's children. If you neglect the conditions appended to them, your heavenly Father will withhold them from you.

The essential blessings of the covenant of grace stand unconditioned. The invitation to seek for mercy is addressed to those who have no qualifications whatsoever except their need. But come inside the divine family as saved men and women, and you will find that other choice blessings are given or withheld according to our attention to the Lord's rules in His family. To give a common illustration: if a hungry person were at your door and asked for bread, you would give it to him, regardless of his character. You will also give your child food, whatever his behavior may be. You will not deny your child anything that is necessary for life. You will never proceed in any course of discipline against him so as to deny him his needful food or clothing to shield him from the cold. But there are many other things that your child may desire that you will give him conditioned upon his obedience. I take it that this illustrates how far the paternal government of God will push this matter and where it will not go.

Understand that the text refers not so much to God's hearing a prayer of His servants, for that God will do even when His servants are not walking with Him and when He is hiding His face from them. But the power in prayer here intended is the continuous and absolute power with God described in the words of the text, "whatsoever we ask, we receive of him."

For this prayer there are certain prerequisites and essentials that should be noted, and the first is *childlike obedience.* "Whatsoever we ask, we receive of him, *because we keep his commandments.*" If we lack this, the Lord may say to us as He did to His people Israel, "Yet have ye forsaken me, and served other gods: wherefore I will deliver you no more. Go and cry unto the gods which ye have chosen" (Judg. 10:13–14). Any father will tell you that for him to grant the request of a disobedient child would be to encourage rebellion in the family and render it impossible for him to rule in his own house. It is often incumbent upon the parent to say, "My child, you do not listen to my word, therefore, I cannot listen to yours." It is not that the father does not love but that he does love the child. Because of his love, the father feels bound to show his displeasure by refusing the request of his erring offspring. God acts with us as we should act toward our stubborn children, and if He sees that we will go into sin and transgress, it is a part of His kind paternal discipline to say, "I will not hear your prayer when you cry to Me. You shall be saved and have the bread and the water of life, but you shall have no more. The luxuries of My kingdom shall be denied you, and anything like special prevailing with Me in prayer you shall not possess."

That the Lord deals with His own people is clear: "Oh that my people had hearkened unto me, and Israel had walked in my ways! I should soon have subdued their enemies, and turned my hand against their adversaries. . . . He should have fed them also with the finest of the wheat: and with honey out of the rock should I have satisfied thee" (Ps. 81:13–14, 16). If the disobedient child of God had the promise put into his hands—"Whatsoever ye ask in prayer, ye shall receive"—he would be sure to ask for something that would support him in his rebellion. He would be asking for provisions for his own lust and aid for his personal rebellion. This can never be tolerated. Shall God be a supplier to our corruptions? Shall He fuel the flames of carnal passion? A self-willed heart hankers after greater liberty that it may be the more obstinate. A haughty spirit longs for greater elevation that it may be prouder still. A slothful spirit asks for greater ease that it may be yet more indolent. A domineering spirit asks for more power that it may have more opportunities of oppression. As is the man, such will his prayer be. Shall God listen to these prayers? It cannot be. He will give us what we ask *if we keep His commandments*, but if we become disobedient and reject His government, He will reject our prayers and say, "And if ye walk contrary unto me, . . . will I also walk contrary unto you" (Lev. 26:21, 24). Happy shall we be if through divine grace we can say with David, "I will wash mine hands in innocency: so will I compass thine altar, O LORD" (Ps. 26:6). This will never be perfect innocency, but it will at least be an innocence of the love of sin and of willful revolt from God.

Next to childlike obedience is another essential to victorious prayer: *childlike reverence*. Notice the next sentence in the text: We receive what we ask "because we keep his commandments, and *do those things that are pleasing in his sight.*" When a child is given a command from his father, we do not let the child question its propriety or wisdom. Obedience ends where questioning begins. A child's standard for obedience must not become the measure of the father's right to command. Good children say, "Father has told us to do this, and therefore we will do it, for we delight to please him always." The strongest reason for a loving child's action is the persuasion that it would please his parents, and the strongest thing that can be said to hold back a gracious child is to prove that such a course of action would displease his parents. It is precisely so with us toward God, who is a perfect parent. We may without fear always make His pleasure the rule of right, while the rule of wrong may safely remain that which would displease Him. Suppose any of us should be self-willed and say, "I shall not do what pleases God. I shall do what pleases myself." Then, observe, what would be the nature of our prayers? Our prayers might then be summed up in the request, "Let me have my own way." And can we expect God to consent to that? Are we to be not only lords over God's heritage but over God Himself? Would you have the Almighty resign the throne to place a proud mortal there? If you have a child in your house who has no respect whatever for his father, will you stoop when he says, "I want to have my own way in all things"? Will you allow him to dictate to you and forget the honor due to you as father? Will you say, "Yes, my dear child, I recognize your importance. You shall be lord in the house, and whatever you ask for you shall have"?

God's house is not run this way. God will not listen to His self-willed children, unless it is to hear them in anger and to answer them in wrath. Remember how He heard the prayer of Israel for flesh, and when the meat was yet in their mouths it became a curse to them (Num. 11:31–33). Many persons are disciplined by obtaining their own desires, even as backsliders are filled with their own devices. We must have a childlike reverence of God, so that we feel, "Lord, if what I ask for does not please You, neither would it please me. My desires are put into Your hands to be corrected. Strike the pen through every petition that I offer that is not right.

And put in whatever I have omitted, even though I might not have desired it had I considered it. Good Lord, if I should have desired it, hear me as if I had desired it. 'Not as I will, but as Thou wilt.' " Now I think you can see that this yielding spirit is essential to continual prevailing with God in prayer. A lack of submission is a sure obstacle to distinction in supplication. The Lord will be reverenced by those who are round about Him. They must have an eye to His pleasure in all that they do and ask, or He will not look upon them with favor.

The text also suggests the necessity of *childlike trust*. "And this is his commandment, that *we should believe on the name of his Son Jesus Christ.*" Everywhere in Scripture, faith in God is spoken of as necessary to successful prayer. We must "believe that [God] is, and that he is a rewarder of them that diligently seek him" (Heb. 11:6), or else we have not prayed at all. In proportion to our faith will be the success of our prayer. It is a standing rule of the kingdom, "According to your faith be it unto you" (Matt. 9:29). Remember how the Holy Spirit speaks by the pen of the Apostle James: "If any of you lack wisdom, let him ask of God, that giveth to all men liberally, and upbraideth not; and it shall be given him. But let him ask in faith, nothing wavering. For he that wavereth is like a wave of the sea driven with the wind and tossed. For let not that man think that he shall receive any thing of the Lord" (James 1:5–7). The text speaks of faith in the name of His Son Jesus Christ, which I understand to mean faith in His declared character, faith in His gospel, faith in the truth concerning His substitution and salvation. Or it may mean faith in the authority of Christ, so that when I plead with God and say, "Do it in the name of Jesus," I mean, "Do for me as You would have done for Jesus, for I am authorized by Him to use His name. Do it for me as You would have done it for Him." He that can pray with faith in the name cannot fail, for the Lord Jesus has said, "If ye ask anything in my name, I will do it."

But there must be faith, and if there is no faith, we cannot expect to be heard. Do you not see that? Let us come back to our family illustration. Suppose a child in the house does not believe his father's word and is constantly saying that he finds his mind full of doubts as to his father's truthfulness. He is not at all ashamed that he should say such a thing, but he rather feels that he ought to be pitied, as if it were an infirmity that he could not avoid. He declares that though he tries to believe his father's promise, yet he cannot. I think a father so distrusted would not be in a great hurry to grant such a son's request. Indeed, it is very probable that the mistrustful son's petitions would be such as could not be complied with, even if his father were willing to do so, since they would amount to a gratification of his own unbelief and a dishonor to his parent. For instance, suppose this child doubts whether his father would provide him with his daily food. He might then come to his father and say, "Father give me enough money to last until I am a man. Quiet my fears, for I am in great anxiety." The father replies, "My son, why should I do that?" And he gets for a reply, "I am very sorry to say it, dear Father, but I cannot trust you. I have such a weak faith in you and your love that I am afraid one of these days you will leave me to starve, and therefore I should like to have something sure in the bank." What father would listen to such a request? You would grieve that thoughts so dishonoring to yourself should pass through the mind of one of your own beloved ones, but you would not—and could not—give way to them.

Let me ask you to apply the parable to yourself. Did you never offer requests that were of much the same character? You have been unable to trust God to give you day by day your daily bread, and therefore you have been craving for what you call "some provision for the future." You want a more trustworthy provider than providence, a better security than God's promise. You are unable to trust your heavenly Father's Word and find a few bonds of some half-bankrupt business far more reliable! You can trust the barons of financial institutions but not the God of the whole earth! In a thousand ways we insult the Lord by imagining the things which are seen to be more substantial than His unseen omnipotence. We ask God to give us at this moment what we do not require at present and may never need at all. The reason for such desires may be found in a disgraceful distrust of Him that makes us imagine that great provisions are needful to ensure our being provided for. Are you not to blame here, and do you expect the Lord to aid your folly? Shall God encourage your distrust? Shall He give you a heap of gold and silver for thieves to steal and chests of garments to feed moths (Matt. 6:19)? Would you have the Lord act as if He admitted the correctness of your suspicions and confessed to unfaithfulness? God forbid! Expect not, therefore, to be heard when your prayer is suggested by an unbelieving heart: "Commit thy way unto the Lord; trust also in him; and he shall bring it to pass" (Ps. 37:5).

The next essential to continued success in prayer is *childlike love*—"That we should believe on the name of his Son Jesus Christ, and *love one another as he gave us commandment.*" The great commandment after faith is love. As it is said of God, "God is love" (1 John 4:8), so may we say that "Christianity is love." If each of us were incarnations of love, we should have attained to the complete likeness of Christ. We should abound in love to God, love to Christ, love to the church, love to sinners, and love to men everywhere. When a man has no love to God, he is in the condition of a child without love to his father. Shall his father promise absolutely to fulfill all the desires of his unloving heart? Of if a child has no love for his brothers and sisters, shall the father trust him with an absolute promise and say, "Ask and it shall be given thee"? The unloving son would impoverish the whole family by his selfish demands. Regardless of all the rest of the household, the son would care only to indulge his own passions. Few Josephs can wear the garment of many colors and not become household tyrants. Who would allow a prodigal to run off with the estate? Who would be so unwise as to place a greedy, domineering brother in the seat of honor above his brethren?

It is obvious that selfishness cannot be trusted with power in prayer. Spirits that love neither God nor men cannot be trusted with great, broad, unlimited promises. If God is to hear us, we must love God and love our fellow men. When we love God, we shall not pray for anything that would not honor God and shall not wish to see anything happen to us that will not also bless our brethren. Our hearts will beat true to God and to His creatures, and we shall not be wrapped up in ourselves. You must get rid of selfishness before God can trust you with the keys of heaven. But when self is dead, God will enable you to unlock His treasures, and, as a prince, you shall have power with God and prevail.

We must have *childlike ways* as well. "*He that keepeth his commandments, dwelleth in him, and he in him.*" It is one of a child's ways to love his home. The child to whose requests his father always listens, loves no place so much as the dear old house where his parents live. And he who loves and keeps God's commandments is said to dwell in God. He has made the Lord his dwelling place and abides in holy familiarity with God. In him our Lord's words are fulfilled, "If ye abide in me, and my words abide in you, ye shall ask what ye will, and it shall be done unto you" (John 15:7). Faith and love, like two cherubic wings, have borne up the believer's soul above the world and carried him near to the throne of God. In that, the believer has become like God, his prayers are such as God can answer; but until he is thus conformed to the divine mind, there must be some limit to the potency of his pleadings. To dwell in God is essential to power with God.

Suppose one of you had a boy who said, "Father, I do not like my home, and I do not care for you or the restraints of family rule. I am leaving home, but I shall return every week and expect that you will give me whatever I ask from you." Will you not say, "My son, if you are so self-willed as to leave my house, can you expect that I will do your bidding? No, my son, if you will not remain with me as a father, I cannot promise you anything." And so is it with God. If we dwell with Him and commune with Him, He will give us all things. If we love Him as He should be loved and trust Him as He should be trusted, He will hear our requests. But if not, it is not reasonable to expect it. Indeed, it would be a slur upon the divine character for Him to fulfill unholy desires and gratify evil whims. "Delight thyself also in the LORD, and he shall give thee the desires of thine heart" (Ps. 37:4), but if you have no delight in God, He will not answer you. He may give you the bread and water of affliction and make your life bitter, but He certainly will not give you what your heart desires.

One thing more. It appears from the text that we must have a *childlike spirit*, for *"hereby we know that he abideth in us, by the Spirit which he hath given us."* What is this but the Spirit of adoption—the Spirit who rules in all the children of God? The willful who think and feel and act differently from God must not expect that God will come round to their way of thinking and feeling and acting. The selfish who are motivated by the spirit of pride or the slothful who are motivated by the love of ease must not expect that God will indulge them. The Holy Spirit—if He rules in us—will subordinate our nature to His own sway, and then the prayers that spring out of our renewed hearts will be in keeping with the will of God, and such prayers will naturally be heard. The same mind must be in us that was also in Christ Jesus, and then we shall be able to say, "I know that thou hearest me always" (John 11:42).

The Prevalence of These Essential Things

If we have *faith* in God, there is no question about God's hearing our prayer. If we can plead in faith the name and blood of Jesus, we must obtain answers of peace. But a thousand objections are suggested. Suppose these prayers concern the laws of nature, then the scientific men are against us. What of that? I do not know any prayer worth praying that does not come into contact with some natural law or other, and yet I believe in prayers being heard. It is said that God will not change the laws of nature for us, and I reply, "Whoever said He would!" The Lord has ways of answering our prayers irrespective of the working of miracles or suspending of laws. God knows how to accomplish His purposes and hear our prayers by I know not what secret means. Perhaps there are other forces and laws that He has arranged to bring into action just at times when prayer also acts—laws just as fixed and forces just as natural as those that our learned theorizers have been able to discover. The wisest men do not know all the laws that govern the universe. We believe that the prayers of Christians are a part of the machinery of providence, cogs in the great wheel of destiny. When God leads His children to pray, He has already set in motion a wheel that is to produce the result prayed for, and the prayers offered are moving as a part of the wheel. God's own order has established that when there is faith in God. God must hear prayer. The verse before the text says, "If our heart condemn us not, then have we confidence toward God. And whatsoever we ask, we receive of him" (1 John 3:21–22). He who has a clear conscience comes to God with confidence, and that confidence of faith insures the answer of his prayer.

Childlike confidence makes us pray as none else can. It causes a man to pray for great things that he would never have asked for if he had not learned this confidence. It also causes him to pray for little things that many people are afraid to ask for, because they have not yet felt toward God the confidence of children. I have often felt that it requires more confidence in God to pray to Him about a little thing than about great things. We imagine that our great things are somehow worthy of God's attention, though in truth they are little enough to Him. And then we think that our little things must be so insignificant that it is an insult to bring them before Him. We need to realize that what is very important to a child may be very small to his parent, and yet the parent measures the thing not from his own point of view but from the child's. You heard your little boy the other day crying bitterly. The cause of the pain was a splinter in his finger. While you did not call in three surgeons to extract it, the splinter was a great thing to that little sufferer. Standing there with eyes all wet through tears of anguish, it never occurred to that boy that his pain was too small a thing for you to care about. What were mothers and fathers made for but to look after the small concerns of little children? And God our Father is a good father who pities us as fathers pity their children. He counts the stars and calls them all by name, yet He heals the broken in heart and binds up their wounds. The same God who kindles the sun has said, "I will not quench the smoking flax" (Matt. 12:20). If you have put your confidence in God, you will take your great things and little things to Him, knowing He will never belie your confidence. He has said that they that trust in Him "shall not be ashamed nor confounded world without end" (Isa. 45:17). Faith must succeed.

Love must succeed, too, since we have already seen that the man who loves in the Christian sense lives in harmony with God. If you confine your love to your own family, you need to realize that God does not so limit His love, and prayers narrowed within your family circle He will disregard. If a man loves his own little self and hopes everybody's crop of wheat will fail so that his own crop will be worth a higher price, he certainly cannot expect the Lord to agree with such mean selfishness. If a man has a heart large enough to embrace all of God's creatures while he still prays specially for the household of faith, his prayers will be after the Divine mind. The man's love and God's goodness run side by side. Though God's love is like a mighty rolling river compared to the man's trickling brook, yet they both run in the same direction and will both come to the same end. God always hears the prayers of a loving man because those prayers are the shadows of His own decrees.

The man of *obedience* is the man whom God will hear. The man's obedient heart leads him to pray humbly and with submission, for he feels it to be his highest desire that the Lord's will should be done. The man of obedient heart prays like a prophet, and his prayers are prophecies. Is he not one with God? Does he not desire and ask for exactly what God intends? How can a prayer shot from such a bow ever fail to reach its target? If your soul is in harmony with God's soul, you will wish God's own wishes. The difficulty is that we do not stay in harmony with God; but if we did, then we should strike the same note as God strikes. And though God's note would sound like thunder and ours as a whisper, yet there would be a perfect unison—the note struck by prayer on earth would coincide with that which sounds forth from the decrees in heaven.

The man who lives in *fellowship with God* will assuredly succeed in prayer. If the man dwells in God, and God dwells in him, he will desire what God desires. The believer in communion with the Lord desires man's good, and so does God. He desires Christ's glory, and so does God. He desires the church's prosperity, and so does God. He desires his life to be an example of holiness, and God desires it, too. That man knows that he has desires that are not according to God's will, but he provides for this defect by always adding to the end of his prayer: "Lord, if I have asked for anything that is not according to Your mind, I ask You to disregard it. And if any wish that I have expressed to you—even though it is the desire that burns in my bosom above all other wishes—is a wish that is not right in Your sight, disregard it, my Father. But in Your infinite love and compassion, do something better for Your servant than Your servant knows how to ask." When a prayer is after that fashion, how can it fail? The Lord looks out of the windows of heaven and sees such a prayer coming to Him, just as Noah saw the dove returning to the ark, and He puts out His hand to that prayer. As Noah plucked the dove into the ark, so God plucks that prayer in and puts it into His own bosom, saying, "You came out of My bosom, and I welcome you back. My Spirit inspired you, therefore will I answer."

Keep in mind that our text speaks of the Christian as being *filled with God's Spirit*. "We know that he abideth in us, by the Spirit which he hath given us." Who knows the mind of a man but the spirit of a man? So, who knows the things of God but the Spirit of God? And if the Spirit of God dwells in us, He tells us what God's mind is. He makes intercession in the saints according to the will of God (Rom. 8:26). It is sometimes imagined that those who always prevail in prayer can pray for what they like, but I can assure you that is not so. You may call upon such a person and ask him to pray for you, but he cannot promise that he will. There are strange restraints placed upon such people of prayer. I heard it said, "I do not know how or why, but I cannot pray effectual fervent prayers in certain cases, though I desire to do so." Like Paul desiring to go into Bithynia and the Spirit restraining Him, so there are requests that we would naturally like to pray, but we are bound in spirit. On the surface, there may be nothing objectionable about the prayer, but the secret of the Lord is with them that fear Him, and He gives secret intimations when and where His chosen may hope to prevail. The Spirit gives you the promise that He will hear your believing prayer, but He does not at the same time give you faith about everything that everybody requests you to pray about. On the contrary, He gives you a discretion, a judgment, and a wisdom, and the Spirit makes intercession in the saints according to the will of God.

Practical Improvements for Prayer

We need to pray for God to send a great blessing on the church at large. Have we the essentials for success? Are we believing on the name of Jesus Christ? Are we full of love to God and one another? The double commandment is that we believe on the name of Jesus Christ and that we love one another. Do we love one another? Are we walking in love? I confess that I am far from perfect in that respect. How often have we done unloving things, thought unloving things, said unloving things, listened to unloving gossip, held back our hand unlovingly when we should have rendered help, and even put forth our hand unlovingly to push down a man who was falling? If in the church of God there is a lack of love, we cannot expect prayer to be heard, for God will say, "You ask for success. What for? To add more to a community that does not already love itself! You ask for conversions. What! To bring in others to join an unloving community?" Do you expect God to save sinners whom you do not love and to convert souls whom you do not care a bit about? The Holy Spirit's great instrument for the conquest of the world is the love of His people for others. The sword of the Spirit, which is the Word of God, is the master weapon, but next to that is the loving care and generous lifestyle of Christians toward others. How much love do we have, or shall I ask how little?

Are we doing that which is pleasing in God's sight? We cannot expect answers to prayer if we are not. Have you been doing what you would like Jesus Christ to see? Is your household ordered in such a way that it pleases God? Suppose Jesus Christ had visited your house this week, uninvited and unexpected: what would He have thought of what He observed? Unless the members of God's church do what is pleasing in God's sight, they bar the door against the success of the prayers of the church. Who wishes to stand in the way of the success of God's church through an inconsistent Christian life?

Do we dwell in God? The text says that if we keep His commandments, God dwells in us and we in Him. Is that how we live throughout the day? In our business are we still with God? A Christian is not to run to God in the morning and again at night, using Him as a shelter and a means to our own ends. We are to dwell in God and live in Him from the rising of the sun until the day's end, making God the center of our lives and walking as in His sight.

Does the Spirit of God motivate us, or is it another spirit? Do we wait upon God and say, "Lord, let Your Spirit tell me what to say and do in this situation. Be Lord of my judgment, subdue my passions, control my impulses, and let Your Spirit guide me. Lord, be soul and life to me, and in the triple kingdom of my spirit, soul, and body, be my supreme Master. In every province of my nature, may Your law be set up and Your will be done." We would have a mighty church if we are all of this mind. God save us as a church from losing His presence! God grant us grace to be strong enough to overcome the evil that surrounds our lives and, having done all, to stand to the praise of the glory of His grace.

*R*emember *that intercessory prayer is the sweetest prayer God ever hears . . . and is exceedingly prevalent. What wonders it has wrought! Intercessory prayer has stopped plagues. It removed the darkness that rested over Egypt, drove away the frogs that leaped upon the land, scattered the lice and locusts that plagued the inhabitants of Zoan, removed the thunder and lightning, stayed all the ravages that God's avenging hand did upon Pharaoh and his people. We know that intercessory prayer healed diseases in the early church. We have evidence of it in old Mosaic times. When Miriam was smitten with leprosy, Moses prayed and the leprosy was removed. Intercessory prayer has raised the dead, for Elijah stretched himself upon the child seven times, and the child sneezed, and the child's soul returned. As to how many souls intercessory prayer has instrumentally saved, only eternity shall reveal it! There is nothing that intercessory prayer cannot do. Believer, you have a mighty engine in your hand—use it well, use it constantly, use it now with faith, and you shall surely prevail.*

Chapter Eight

Intercessory Prayer

And the LORD turned the captivity of Job, when he prayed for his friends—Job 42:10.

"AND THE LORD TURNED the captivity of Job." What a promise is contained in this verse! Our longest sorrows have an ending, and there is a bottom to the profoundest depths of misery. Winter shall not frown forever; summer shall soon smile. The tide shall not eternally ebb out; the floods retrace their march. The night shall not hang its darkness forever over our souls; the sun shall yet arise with healing beneath his wings.

"And the LORD turned the captivity of Job." Our sorrows shall have an end when God has accomplished His purpose in them. One of the purposes in the case of Job was that Satan might be defeated—foiled with his own weapons and blasted in his hopes when he had everything his own way. In answer to Satan's challenge, God had stretched forth His hand and touched Job in his bone and flesh, and yet the tempter could not prevail against Job. Instead, Satan received his rebuff in those conquering words: "Though he slay me, yet will I trust in him" (Job 13:15). When Satan is defeated, then shall the battle cease.

The Lord aimed also at the trial of Job's faith. Many weights were hung upon this palm tree, but it still grew uprightly. The fire had been fierce enough, the gold was undiminished, and only the dross was consumed.

Another purpose the Lord had was His own glory. And God was glorified abundantly. Job had glorified God while he suffered on the dunghill; now let him magnify his Lord again upon his royal seat in the gate. God had received eternal renown through that grace by which He supported His poor afflicted servant under the heaviest troubles that ever fell to the lot of man.

God had still another end, and that was Job's sanctification through his afflictions. Job's spirit had been mellowed. The small degree of tartness toward others that may have been in Job's temperament had been at last removed, and any self-justification that once lurked within was fairly driven out. Now God's gracious designs are answered, He removes the rod from His servant's back and takes the melted silver from the midst of the glowing coals. God does not willingly afflict or grieve the children of men for nothing. He shows this by the fact that He never afflicts them longer than there is a need for it and never suffers them to be one moment longer in the furnace than is absolutely requisite to serve the purpose of His wisdom and love.

"And the LORD turned the captivity of Job." Beloved brother in Christ, you have had a long captivity in affliction. God has sold you into the hand of your adversaries, and you have wept by the waters of Babylon, hanging your harp upon the willows. Despair not! He who turned the captivity of Job can turn yours as the streams in the south. He shall make your vineyard to blossom and your field to yield her fruit again. You shall again come forth with those who rejoice, and once more shall the song of gladness be on your lips. Let not despair rivet its cruel fetters about your soul. Hope yet, for there *is* hope. Trust thou still, for there is ground of confidence. He shall bring you up from the land of your captivity, and you shall say of Him, "Thou hast turned for me my mourning into dancing" (Ps. 30:11).

The circumstance that accompanied Job's restoration is that to which I invite your particular attention. "And the LORD turned the captivity of Job, when he prayed for his friends." Intercessory prayer was the sign of Job's returning greatness. It was the rainbow in the cloud, the dove bearing the olive branch, the voice of the turtle announcing the coming summer. When Job's soul began to expand itself in holy and loving prayer for his erring brethren, the heart of God showed itself to him by returning his prosperity and cheering his soul within. What lessons on the subject of prayer for others are contained in such a text as this. Let us learn to imitate the example of Job and pray for our friends.

Four things stand out to me concerning intercessory prayer. First, *the exercise of intercessory prayer is highly commended.* Second, *we are encouraged to enlist in it.* Third, *it is suggested as to whom we should pray for.* Fourth, *all believers are exhorted to persevere in the exercise of intercession for others.*

Intercessory Prayer Commended

Let me remind you that intercessory prayer has been *practiced by all the best of God's saints.* We may not find instances of it appended to every saint's name, but there has never been a saint eminent for godliness who has not always been preeminent in his anxious desires for the good of others and in his prayers for that end. Take Abraham, the father of the faithful. How earnestly did he plead for his son Ishmael! "O that Ishmael might live before thee!" (Gen. 17:18). With what importunity did he approach the Lord on the plains of Mamre when he wrestled with Him again and again for Sodom. "Wilt thou also destroy the righteous with the wicked? Peradventure there be fifty. . . . Peradventure there shall lack five of the fifty. . . . Peradventure there shall be twenty found there. . . . Peradventure ten shall be found there" (Gen. 18:23–32). Well did he intercede, and if we may sometimes be tempted to wish he had not paused when he did, yet we must commend him for continuing so long to plead for that doomed and depraved city.

Remember Moses, the most royal of men, how often did he intercede! How frequently do you meet with such a record as this—"Moses and Aaron fell on their faces" (Numb. 14:5). Remember that cry of Moses on the top of the mount when it was to his own personal disadvantage to intercede. When God had said, "Let me alone . . . I will make of thee a great nation" (Ex. 32:10), yet how Moses continued, how he thrust himself in the way of the ax of justice and cried, "If thou wilt forgive their sin—; and if not," (and here he reached the very climax of agonizing earnestness) "blot me, I pray thee, out of thy book" (Ex. 32:32). Never was there a mightier prophet than Moses and never one more intensely earnest in intercessory prayer.

Or pass on to the days of Samuel. Remember his words, "God forbid that I should sin against the LORD in ceasing to pray for you" (1 Sam. 12:23). Or think of Solomon and his earnest intercession with outstretched hands as he prayed for the assembled people at the opening of the temple (1 Kings 8). Turn to Hezekiah with Sennacherib's letter spread out before the Lord, when he prayed not only for himself but also for God's people of Israel in those times of trouble (2 Kings 19:14). Think of Elijah, who for Israel's sake would bring down the rain that the land would not perish. As for himself, miracles gave Elijah his bread and his water, but it was for others that he prayed and said to his servant, "Go again seven times" (1 Kings 18:43). Forget not Jeremiah whose tears were prayers—prayers coming too intensely from his heart to find expression in any utterance of the lip (Jer. 13:17). Jeremiah's life was one long shower, each drop a prayer, and the whole deluge a flood of intercession. And if you would have an example taken from the times of Christ and His apostles, recall Peter praying on the top of the house or Stephen amidst the falling stones. Or think of Paul, who said that he never ceased to remember the saints in his prayers, making "mention of you always in my prayers" (Rom. 1:9), stopping in the very midst of the epistle and saying, "For this cause I bow my knees unto the Father of our Lord Jesus Christ" (Eph. 3:14).

While we might commend this duty of intercessory prayer by quoting innumerable examples from the lives of eminent saints, it is enough for the disciple of Christ if we say that *Christ has specified it as our duty and privilege* to intercede for others. When He taught us to pray, He said, "*Our* Father," and the expressions that follow are not in the singular but in the plural: "Give *us* this day *our* daily bread . . . Forgive *us our* debts . . . Lead *us* not into temptation" (Matt. 6:9–13). Evidently, He intended to show that none of us are to pray for ourselves alone. While we may have prayers so bitter that they must be personal like the Savior's own—"O my Father, if it be possible, let this cup pass from me" (Matt. 26:39)—yet, as a rule, our prayers should not forget the church of the living God.

By the pen of Paul how frequently does the Holy Ghost exhort us to pray for ministers! "Brethren," says Paul, "pray for us" (2 Thess. 3:1). James, the ever practical apostle, bids us, "Confess your faults one to another, and pray one for another, that ye may be healed" (James 5:16), as if the healing would come not only to the sick person for whom we pray but also to us who offer the prayer. We, too, receive some special blessing when our hearts are enlarged for the people of the living God.

But I shall not stay to quote the texts in which the duty of praying for others is definitely laid down. Permit me to remind you of *the high example of your Master*. Jesus is your pattern; follow His leadership. Was there even one who interceded as He did? Remember His golden prayer where He cried to the Father for His own people: "keep them from the evil" (John 17:15). What a prayer was that! Jesus seems to have thought of all their needs and weaknesses, and in one long stream of intercession, He pours out His heart before His Father's throne. Consider that even in the agonies of His crucifixion, He did not forget that He was still an intercessor for man. "Father, forgive them; for they know not what they do" (Luke 23:34). And remember that it is your Savior who is today before the throne with outstretched hands praying for you—the purchase of His blood—and for those who shall believe on Him through your word. With such an example as this, we are truly guilty if we forget to plead for others.

If in the Bible there were no examples of intercession, if Christ had not left it upon record that it was His will that we should pray for others, and even if we did not know that it was Christ's practice to intercede, yet *the very spirit of our holy faith* would constrain us to plead for others. Do you go into prayer and in the face and presence of God not thinking of anyone but yourself? Surely the love of Christ cannot be in you, for the Spirit of Christ is not selfish. No man lives unto himself when once he has the love of Christ in him. I know there are some whose religion is comfortably tethered within the limits of their own selfish interests. It is enough for them if *they* heard the Word, if *they* are saved, if *they* get to heaven. Ah, miserable spirit, you shall not get there! It would require another heaven for you, for the heaven of Christ is the heaven of the unselfish, the temple of the large hearts, the bliss of loving spirits. It is the heaven of those who, like Christ, are willing to become poor that others may be rich. I cannot believe—it is a scandal upon the doctrine which He taught—that the man whose prayers are selfish has anything of the Spirit of Christ within him. I commend intercessory prayer because it opens man's soul, bringing a healthy play to his sympathies and constraining him to feel that he is not everybody. It convinces the man that this wide world and this great universe were not made that he might be its petty lord, that everything might bend to his will, and all creatures crouch at his feet. It does him good, I say, to make him know that the cross was not uplifted alone for him, for its far-reaching arms were meant to drop with benedictions upon millions of the human race. To the lean and hungry worshipper of self, intercessory prayer would make another man of you, a man more like the Son of Man and less like Nabal the churl (1 Sam. 25).

I commend the blessed privilege of intercession because of its sweet brotherly nature. You and I may be naturally hard, harsh, and unlovely of spirit, but praying for others will remind us we have, indeed, a relationship to the saints—that their interests are ours, that we are jointly concerned with them in all the privileges of grace. I do not know anything that through the grace of God may be a better means of uniting us to one another than constant prayer for each other. You cannot harbor enmity in your soul against your brother after you have learned to pray for him. If he has done you wrong, when you have taken that wrong to the mercy seat and prayed over it, you must forgive. Surely you could not be such a hypocrite as to invoke blessings on his head before God and then come forth to curse him in your own soul. When there have been complaints brought by brother against brother, it is generally best to say, "Let us pray before we enter into the matter." If you will exercise yourselves much in supplication for your brethren, you will forgive their tempers, you will overlook their rashness, you will not think of their harsh words; but knowing that you also may be tempted and are of like passions with them, you will cover their faults and bear with their weaknesses.

To add one more commendation of intercessory prayer, it seems to me that when God gives any man much grace, it must be with the design that he may use it for the rest of the family. I would compare you who have close communion with God to courtiers in the king's palace. What do courtiers do? Do they not avail themselves of their influence at court to take the petitions of their friends and present them where they can be heard? There is a kind of heavenly patronage that you should exercise diligently. I ask you to use it on the behalf of your minister. Use it on the behalf of the poor, the sick, the afflicted, the tempted, the tried, the desponding, the despairing. When you have the King's ear, speak to Him for others. When you are permitted to come very near to His throne, when your faith is strong, your eye clear, your interest sure, and the love of God sweetly shed abroad in your heart—then take the petitions of your poor brethren who stand outside at the gate. It is utterly impossible that you should have a large measure of grace unless it prompts you to use your influence for others. If your soul has grace at all and you are not a mighty intercessor, that grace must be but as a grain of mustard seed—a shrivelled, puny thing. You have just enough grace to float your soul clear from the quicksand, but you have no deep floods of grace or else you would carry a rich cargo of the needs of others up to the throne of God. And you would bring back for them rich blessings that they might not have obtained without you. If you are like an angel with your foot upon the golden ladder that reaches to heaven, if you are ascending and descending, know that you will ascend with others' prayers and descend with others' blessings, for it is impossible for a mature saint to live or to pray for himself alone.

Encouragement to Intercession

Remember that intercessory prayer is the sweetest prayer God ever hears. Do not question it, for the prayer of Christ is of this character. In all the incense that our Great High Priest now puts into the censer, there is not a single grain that is for Himself. His work is done, His reward obtained. Now you do not doubt that Christ's prayer is the most acceptable of all supplications. Thus, the more your prayer is like Christ's, the sweeter it will be. And while petitions for yourself will be accepted, yet your pleadings for others—having in them more of the fruits of the Spirit, more love, perhaps more faith, certainly more brotherly kindness—will be as the sweetest sacrifice that you can offer to God. Remember, again, that intercessory prayer is exceedingly prevalent. What wonders it has wrought! Intercessory prayer has stopped plagues. It removed the darkness that rested over Egypt, drove away the frogs that leaped upon the land, scattered the lice and locusts that plagued the inhabitants of Zoan, removed the thunder and lightning, stayed all the ravages that God's avenging hand did upon Pharaoh and his people. We know that intercessory prayer healed diseases in the early church. We have evidence of it in old Mosaic times. When Miriam was smitten with leprosy, Moses prayed and the leprosy was removed. Intercessory prayer has raised the dead, for Elijah stretched himself upon the child seven times, and the child sneezed, and the child's soul returned. As to how many souls intercessory prayer has instrumentally saved, only eternity shall reveal it! There is nothing that intercessory prayer cannot do. Believer, you have a mighty engine in your hand—use it well, use it constantly, use it now with faith, and you shall surely prevail.

Perhaps you have a doubt about interceding for someone who has fallen far into sin. Did you ever hear of men who have been thought to be dead while yet alive? Have you never heard some old-fashioned story of one who was wrapped up in his shroud to be put into his coffin, and yet he was but in a trance and not dead? I cannot vouch for the accuracy of those tales, but I can tell you that spiritually there has been many a man given up for dead who was still within reach of grace. God found them and took them out of the horrible pit and out of the miry clay, setting their living feet upon His living rock. Never give up anyone for spiritually dead until they are lain out for dead naturally. But perhaps you say, "I cannot pray for others, for I am so weak, so powerless." You will gain strength by the exercise. But besides, the prevalence of prayer depends not upon the strength of the man who prays but upon the power of the argument he uses. If you sow seed, you may be very feeble, but it is not your hand that produces the harvest—it is the vitality of the seed. And so in the prayer of faith. When you can plead a promise and drop that prayer into the ground with hope, your weakness shall not make it miscarry. It shall still prevail with God and bring down blessings from on high. Job came from his dunghill to intercede, and so may I come from my couch of weakness. You come from your poverty to intercede for others, and so may we. Elijah was a man of like passions, weaknesses, and tendencies to sin, but he prevailed. And so shall you if you are not negligent in these exercises but you pray much for others even as Job prayed for his friends.

For Whom We Should Intercede

In the case of Job, he prayed for his *offending* friends. They had spoken exceedingly harshly of him. They had misconstrued all his previous life, and though there had never been a part of his character that deserved censure—for the Lord witnessed concerning him that he was a perfect and an upright man—yet they accused him of hypocrisy, supposing that all he did was for the sake of gain. Perhaps there is no greater offense that can be given to an upright and a holy man than to suspect his motives and to accuse him of self-seeking. And yet, shaking off everything, as the sun forgets the darkness that has hidden its glory and scatters it by its own beams, Job comes to the mercy seat and pleads. He is accepted himself, and he begs that his friends may be accepted, too. Carry your offending ones to the throne of God. It shall be a blessed method of proving the trueness of your forgiveness. When you are alone before God—not that you may gratify your revenge by telling the story out again—ask the Lord to forgive your erring brother and to remove any sin that may have stained his garments.

Be sure you bring your *argumentative* friends. These brethren had been arguing with Job, and the controversy dragged its weary length along. It is better to pray than it is to argue. Sometimes you think it would be a good thing to have a public discussion upon a doctrine. It would be a better thing to have prayer over it. Carry your dear friends who are wrong in practice—not to the discussion room—before God, and let this be your cry, "Teach me if I am wrong, and teach my friend wherein *he* errs, and make him right."

This is the thing we ought also to do with our *haughty* friends. Eliphaz and Bildad were very proud. How they looked down upon poor Job! They thought he was a very great sinner, a very desperate hypocrite. They stayed with him, but doubtless they thought it a very great condescension. You sometimes hear complaints made by Christians about other people being proud. It will not make them humble for you to grumble about it. What if there is a brother who will not notice you in the street because you happen to be poor? The best thing is to tell your Father about it. You would not be angry with a man for having a cataract in the eye—you would pity him. Why be angry with your brother because of his being proud? It is a disease, a very bad disease, that scarlet fever of pride. Go and pray the Lord to cure him, for your anger will not do it. Your anger may puff him up and make him worse than ever he was before, but it will not set him right. Pray him down, brother, pray him down. Have a duel with him, choosing the weapon of all-prayer. If he is proud, I know this, if you prevail with God, God will soon take the pride out of His own child and make him humble as he should be.

Particularly let me ask you to pray most for those who are *disabled from praying* for themselves. Job's three friends could not pray for themselves because the Lord said He would not accept them if they did. God said He was angry with them, but as for Job, said he, "Him will I accept" (Job 42:8). Do not let me shock your feelings when I say there are some—even of God's people—who are not able to pray acceptably at certain seasons. When a man has been committing sin, repentance is his first work, not prayer. He must first set matters right between God and his own soul before he may go and intercede for others. And there are many Christians who cannot pray. Doubt has come in, sin has taken away their confidence, and they are standing outside the gate with their petitions. They dare not enter within the veil. There are many tried believers, too, who are so depressed that they cannot pray with faith, and therefore they cannot prevail. If you can pray, take their sins into court with you, and when you have had your own hearing, then say, "But, my Lord, inasmuch as You have honored me with Your presence, hear me for Your poor people who are just now denied the light of Your countenance." Besides, there are millions of poor sinners who are dead in sin and cannot pray. Pray for *them*. It is a blessed thing—that vicarious repentance and vicarious faith—that a saint may exert toward a sinner. "Lord, that sinner does not feel; help me to feel for him because he will not feel. Lord, that sinner will not believe in Christ. He does not think that Christ can save him, but I know He can. I will pray believingly for that sinner, and I will repent for him, and though my repentance and faith will not avail him without his personal repentance and faith, yet it may come to pass that through me he may be brought to repentance and led to prayer."

Exhortations to Pray for Others

Do you always pray for others? Do you think you have taken the case of your children, your church, your neighborhood, and the ungodly world before God as you should have done? If *you* have, *I* have not. I writes this as a chief culprit before the Master to make confession of the sin, and while I shall exhort you to practice what is undoubtedly a noble privilege, I shall be most of all exhorting myself.

How can you and I repay the debt we owe to the church unless we pray for others? How was it that you were converted? It was because somebody else prayed for you. In tracing back my own conversion, I cannot fail to impute it to the prayers of my mother through the Spirit of God. I believe that the Lord heard her earnest cries when I did not know that her soul was exercised about me. You may have been prayed for when you were asleep in your cradle as an infant. Your mother's liquid prayers fell hot upon your infant brow and gave you what was a true *christening* while you were still but little. Perhaps you are a husband who owes his conversion to his wife's prayers. Perhaps it was the prayers of a sister or a Sunday school teacher. If by others' prayers you and I were brought to Christ, how can we repay this Christian kindness but by pleading for others? He who has not a man to pray for him may write himself down a hopeless character. Let no man of your acquaintance say that there is nobody to pray for him. As you had somebody to plead for you, let poor souls of your acquaintance find in you a person to plead for them.

How are you to prove your love to Christ or to His church if you refuse to pray for men? "We know that we have passed from death unto life, because we love the brethren" (1 John 3:14). If we do not love the brethren, we are still dead. I will say no man loves the brethren who does not pray for them. It is the very least thing you can do, and if you do not perform the least, you certainly will fail in the greater. Let me ask you again, How is it that you hope to get your own prayers answered if you never plead for others?

Will not the Lord say, "Selfish wretch, you are always knocking at my door, but it is always to cry for your own welfare and never for another's. Inasmuch as you have never asked for a blessing for one of the least of these my brethren, neither will I give a blessing to you. If you love not the saints or your fellow men, how can you love Me whom you have not seen? And how shall I love you and give you the blessing that you ask at My hands?"

I earnestly exhort you to intercede for others, for how can you be a Christian if you do not? Christians are priests, but how are they priests if they offer no sacrifice? Christians are lights, but how are they lights unless they shine for others? Christians are sent into the world, even as Christ was sent into the world, but how are they sent unless they are sent to pray? Not only are Christians to be blessed themselves, but in them shall all the nations of the earth be blessed.

Let your prayers unite with one heart and with one soul to plead with God for your neighborhood! Carry the names of your neighbors written on your breast just as the high priest of old carried the names of the tribes. Mothers, bear your children before God! Fathers, carry your sons and daughters! Let us intercede for a wicked world and the dark places thereof that are full of the habitations of cruelty! Let us cry aloud and keep no silence, giving the Lord no rest till He establish and make His church a praise in the earth. Wake you watchmen upon Zion's walls and renew your shouts! The cloud hangs above you—it is yours to draw down its sacred floods in genial showers by earnest prayers. God has put high up in the mountains of His promise springs of love—it is yours to bring them down by the divine channel of your intense supplications. Let us be Christians. Let us have expanded souls and minds that can feel for others. Let us weep with them that weep and rejoice with them that rejoice, and as a church and as private persons, we shall find the Lord will turn our captivity when we pray for our friends.

No matter what level of spiritual maturity we are on, we need renewed appearances, fresh manifestations, new visitations from on high. While it is right to thank God for the past and look back with joy to His visits to you in your early days as a believer, I encourage you to seek God for special visitations of His presence. I do not mean to minimize our daily walk in the light of His countenance; but consider that though the ocean has its high tides twice every day, yet it also has its spring tides. The sun shines whether we see it or not, even through our winter's fog, and yet it has its summer brightness. If we walk with God constantly, there are special seasons when He opens the very secret of His heart to us and manifests Himself to us—not only as He does not to the world but also as He does not at all times to His own favored ones. Not every day in a palace is a banqueting day, and not all days with God are so clear and glorious as certain special sabbaths of the soul in which the Lord unveils His glory. Happy are we if we have once beheld His face, but happier still if He comes to us again in the fullness of favor.

Chapter Nine

Essential Points in Prayer

That the LORD appeared to Solomon the second time, as he had appeared unto him at Gibeon. And the LORD said unto him, I have heard thy prayer and thy supplication, that thou hast made before me: I have hallowed this house, which thou hast built, to put my name there for ever; and mine eyes and mine heart shall be there perpetually—1 Kings 9:2–3.

IT WAS AN EXCEEDINGLY ENCOURAGING thing to Solomon that the Lord should appear to him before the beginning of his great work of building the temple. In 1 Kings 3:5 we read: "In Gibeon the LORD appeared to Solomon in a dream by night: and God said, Ask what I shall give thee." Some of us remember how the Lord was with us at the beginning of our life-work. We started as young men and women newly converted, full of zeal and earnestness, determined to do something for the Lord. How we sought His face! With what simplicity, with what tenderness of heart, with what dependence upon Him and diffidence as to ourselves! We remember, as He remembers, the love of those early days. I cannot forget when the Lord first appeared to me in my own personal Gibeon. Truly there are things about our Christian lives that would not have been possible had God not appeared to us at the beginning. Had He not strengthened and taught us, giving us wisdom beyond what we possess naturally, where would we be? Had He not inspirited us, infusing His very life into us, we would not have done what we have already done. It is a priceless blessing to begin with God and to not lay a stone of the temple of our life work till the Lord has appeared to us.

I wonder, however, if it is perhaps a superior blessing for the Lord to appear to us after a certain work is done. Take the example of our text: "That the LORD appeared to Solomon the second time, as he had appeared unto him at Gibeon." Solomon had just finished the temple work, and he needed another visit from on high. There is great joy in completing a work, and yet many people experience a great emotional drop when the once engrossing service ceases to keep the mind stretched to the limit. You run uphill and gain the summit, but then you almost wish that you had to struggle again when there is no climbing. A work like that of Solomon lasting for seven years must have become a delight to him—seeing the house growing and marking all the stages of its beauty. And so it is with any special and notable work that we are called to do early in our Christian life. We get wedded to it and are glad to see it grow under our hand, yet when our particular portion of service is finished, we feel a kind of loss. We have grown used to the pull upon the collar, we have almost leaned upon it, and we feel a difference when we are at the top of the hill. Rather than feeling exhilarated at a successful Christian service, I experience a certain sinking of heart when the tug of war is over. We see this principle in the story of several of God's great servants. I note it particularly in Elijah when he had performed his mighty work on Carmel and slain the prophets of Baal. He felt an exultation in his spirit for a while, and he ran before the chariot of the king in the joy of his soul. But there came a reaction afterward of a very painful kind. The case of Solomon is not parallel, and yet I think that Solomon was in a condition of special need when the temple was finished. He may have been in peril of pride, if not of depression. In either case it was a remarkable season, and its need must have been remarkable also, "that the LORD appeared to Solomon the second time, as he had appeared unto him at Gibeon."

No matter what level of spiritual maturity we are on, we need renewed appearances, fresh manifestations, new visitations from on high. While it is right to thank God for the past and look back with joy to His visits to you in your early days as a believer, I encourage you to seek God for special visitations of His presence. I do not mean to minimize our daily walk in the light of His countenance, but consider that though the ocean has its high tides twice every day, yet it also has its spring tides. The sun shines whether we see it or not, even through our winter's fog, and yet it has its summer brightness. If we walk with God constantly, there are special seasons when He opens the very secret of His heart to us and manifests Himself to us—not only as He does not to the world but also as He does not at all times to His own favored ones. Not every day in a palace is a banqueting day, and not all days with God are so clear and glorious as certain special sabbaths of the soul in which the Lord unveils His glory. Happy are we if we have once beheld His face, but happier still if He comes to us again in the fullness of favor.

I commend you to be seeking God's second appearances. We should be crying to God most pleadingly that He would speak to us a second time. We do not need a reconversion, as some assert. If the Lord has kept us steadfast in His fear, we are already possessors of what some call the higher life. This we are privileged to enjoy from the first hour of our spiritual life. We do not need to be converted again, but we do need the windows of heaven to be opened again and again over our heads. We need the Holy Spirit to be given again as at Pentecost and that we should renew our youth like the eagles, to run without weariness and walk without fainting. May the Lord fulfill to His people His blessing upon Solomon! "That the LORD appeared to Solomon the second time, as he had appeared unto him at Gibeon."

What the Lord spoke upon the commencement of His interview with Solomon concerned his prayer. And as the Lord answered Solomon's prayer and here—in this second appearance—recounted the points of it, we may be sure that there was much about the prayer that makes it a model for us. We shall do well to pray after the manner that successful intercessors have set. In this case, we will follow the Lord's own description of an accepted prayer.

Our Proper Place in Prayer

"And the LORD said unto him, I have heard thy prayer and thy supplication, that thou hast made *before me*." The place to pray is clearly before the Lord. But we should take care that the place is hallowed by our prayer deliberately and reverently presented before God.

This place is not always found. The Pharisee went up to the temple to pray (Luke 18:9), and yet, evidently, he did not pray "before God." Even in the most holy courts, the Pharisee did not find the place desired. The Pharisee prayed in his own esteem, but his leaving the temple without justification was evidence that he either had not prayed at all or had not prayed before God. It is not because you enter a church and sit in a pew that you are before God. To seek the shrines that have been most eminently regarded by the church, to stand by the site of that little skull-like hill called Calvary and pray there, to go to Olivet and bow your knee in Gethsemane, does not necessarily bring you before God. The nearer we are to the church, sometimes, the farther we are from God. We can be in the very center of the prayer meeting and not be "before God" at all. Praying before God is a more spiritual business than is performed by merely turning to the east or to the west or bowing the knee or entering within walls hallowed for ages. Unfortunately, it is easy enough to pray and not to pray before God. And it is not so easy—it is indeed a thing not to be done except by the power of the Holy Spirit—to "entereth into that within the veil" (Heb. 6:19) and to stand before the mercy seat—consciously and really in the presence of the Invisible, fulfilling the precept, "Ye people, pour out your heart before him" (Ps. 62:8). "Before him" is the place for the soul's outpouring, and blessed is anyone who finds it!

This blessed place "before God" *can be found in public prayer.* Solomon's prayer before God was offered in the midst of a great multitude. The priests stood in their places, and the Levites kept their due order. The people were gathered together, and all the armies of the tribes of Israel stood in the streets of the holy city when Solomon bowed his knee and cried mightily to his God. It is evident that Solomon did not pray to please the people or to impress them with his eloquent language and marvelous performance. Solomon was inspired to pray before the Lord.

Those of us who lead others in public prayer should strive diligently that we may be seen of God in secret when heard of men in public. And I am sure that we pray far more powerfully and effectively for others when we are surrounded as with a cloud, enclosed within the secret place of the Most High, than when we stand praying aloud in the public assembly of God's people. The same is true for every Christian. It is wrong for you to pray in a meeting with a motive to impress an individual of importance or with the remembrance of those present whose respect you would like to obtain. The mercy seat is no place for the exhibition of your abilities. An even greater evil is to use public prayer as an opportunity for making personal remarks about others. I have often heard oblique hints being given in prayer. I am sorry to say that I have even heard remarks that were so directly critical and offensive of others that I lamented it. Such a proceeding is altogether objectionable and irreverent. We do not even pray in prayer meetings to correct doctrinal errors or to teach biblical truth or to remark upon the errors of certain brethren or to impeach them before the Most High. These concerns should be serious matters of supplication but not of a sort of indirect preaching and scolding in prayer. It is conduct worthy of the accuser of the brethren to turn prayer into an opportunity for finding fault with others. Our prayer must be "before God" to be an acceptable prayer. If our eyes and memories and thoughts can be shut to the presence of everybody else, it is in the presence of God that we truly pray—and that, I say, may be done in public, if grace is given. For this we have need to pray, "O Lord, open thou my lips: and my mouth shall shew forth thy praise" (Ps. 51:15).

Prayer before God can just as well—perhaps more readily—*be offered in private*, though I fear that true prayer is easily missed even there. Perhaps you are familiar with the following scene. You are in private prayer and find yourself repeating spiritual words while your heart is wandering. Most of us have found that our prayers have simply become a matter of habit, resulting in as much being said before the walls of our room as before God. We have not realized His presence. We have not spoken distinctly and directly to Him. It is possible that you are observing the Savior's teaching by shutting the door in private prayer, and yet you find that you have mainly prayed in your own presence and God has been far away from your inmost soul. It is poor work merely to talk piously to yourself. "I pour out my soul in me," says David (Ps. 42:4). There is not much that comes of pouring your heart into your own heart, praying your soul into your own soul. It is neither an emptying of self nor a filling with God. It only stirs up what might as well have been left as dregs at the bottom.

Better far is the course prescribed in that hallowed precept: "Ye people, pour out your heart before him" (Ps. 62:8). Turn your prayers upward and let them completely run out before God, leaving room in your heart for something better and more divine. Pouring out your soul within yourself does not come to much, and yet that may be about all that your prayer amounts to—a personal recapitulation of desires without a grasp of divine supplies, a bemoaning of weakness without a reception of strength, a consciousness of nothingness without a plunging into all-sufficiency. Let us remember that the main point of supplication is not to pray in the presence of others or in your own presence but to present your prayer before God.

It is clear that this means that *the prayer is to be directed to God*. That sounds so simple, and yet how often we forget it. Like a playful child, we get our bow and arrows and shoot them anywhere. The way to true prayer is to take the bow and arrows in hand but not shoot with them with all your might in such haste. Wait a bit! Yes, draw the string and fit the arrow to it, but wait, wait! Wait till you have your eye fixed on the target! Wait till you see the center of the mark distinctly! Why shoot if you have nothing to shoot at? Wait, then, till you know what you are going to do. Focus on the center of the target. Imitate David's admonition for prayer: "In the morning will I direct my prayer unto thee, and will look up" (Ps. 5:3). He has fixed the arrow, drawn the bow, and taken deliberate aim, then he lets the arrow fly. He caught the mark with his eye, and therefore he has struck it with his arrow. Oh, to pray with a distinct object!

Indefinite praying is a waste of breath. To begin praying simply because the time has come for it will never do. We must think, *I am about to ask God for what I desire. I am to speak to the great King of kings from whom all grace must come. It is to Him that my prayer must be directed. What, then, shall I ask from His hands?* Does the repeating of certain words out of a book or of our own making have any virtue in it? Some seem—by their frequent repetitions of the Lord's Prayer—to think that there is a magical charm in that sacred arrangement of words. I tell you solemnly that you might as well repeat that perfect prayer backward as forward, if your heart is not in it. If your soul is not looking Godward, you profane the Lord's words and are guilty of all the greater sin because of their excellence. True praying does not resemble the mindless chants of a wizard. Pray distinctly to your God with all your faculties. Speak to Him.

It becomes essential that *we should endeavor in prayer to realize the presence of God*. It may be stated this way: you have prayed well if you have spoken to God as a man speaks to his friend. If you are as sure that God is there as that you are there, and perhaps somewhat more sure; if you are in Him, and He is in you; and if you talk to Him as to one whom you cannot see but can perceive better than by sight, you have prayed well. If you speak to Him as to one whom you cannot feel with your hand but can feel with all your inner nature, knowing that He is hearing you and will reward your diligent seeking, this is praying and pleading before a living God who feels and is moved by what you feel. You are to commune with a tender God who is sensitive to all the sensations of your soul. Oh, to know the meaning of coming before the living and acting God! He is neither a lame and impotent God nor an impersonal and dead God, but He is the true God—God in Christ Jesus! If we know who He is to whom we speak—God, very nigh to us in the person of the Only Begotten, who has taken our nature upon Himself—what praying ours would be! And that is the right sort of praying. Oh, that the God of truth may be able—in speaking to each of us—to say concerning us as He did to Solomon, "I have heard thy prayer and thy supplication, that thou hast prayed before me"! Lord, help us to pass through the outer courts and to enter into Your inner court and speak with You. Lord, deliver us from staying in the words of our prayers, but may You be brought into the spirit of praying.

Do you desire to enter into true prayer? Do not ask, "What shall I say?" Say to God what you wish to say. What is your desire? Would you be saved? Beg Him to save you. Would you be forgiven? Ask forgiveness. "The words," you say, "tell me the words." Nay, you need no words. If you have none, look, look to Him. Let your heart think out its desires. There is music without words, and there is prayer without words. The soul of prayer is *being before* God and *desiring before* God. He hears without sounds and understands without expressions. Open your heart, look to Him, and ask Him to read what you cannot read. Beg Him of His great mercy to give you, not according to your own sense of your requirements but according to the riches of His mercy in Christ Jesus. You are praying before God when you have realized His presence. The Lord does not require that you should express yourself in words. He reads what is written on your heart with an omniscient glance. To know that He knows your heart and to plead in that spirit is prayer before God.

Our Great Goal in Prayer

Our great desire in prayer is that which God said that He had given to Solomon. "I have heard thy prayer and thy supplication."

I have often said that today's wise men—whose principal characteristic is that they think so much of themselves and so very little of anybody else—tell us that prayer is an excellent exercise, good and comforting and useful. But they add that we are not to suppose that prayer has any effect upon God whatsoever. We inquire of them, "Would you have us go on praying after the information you have given?" "Of course," they say, "it is a pious exercise, a proper and edifying thing. Go on praying, but do not think that God hears." It is evident that they think us idiots. Evidently they consider praying men to be born fools. If prayer has no effect upon God, I may as well whistle when I rise in the morning as to pray, and I would as soon close my eyes at night in silence as run over a set of ineffectual words. There is no benefit in prayer if it never goes beyond the room in which it is uttered. When it ceases to be accepted by the Lord and honored by His response, we should abandon it. If there is neither hearing nor answering, we shall have reduced ourselves to the level of pathetic worshippers of Baal (1 Kings 18). But we have not come to that yet.

What we desire in prayer is an *audience with God*. If the Lord does not hear us, we have gained nothing. And what an honor it is to have an audience with God! The frail, feeble, undeserving creature is permitted to stand in the august presence of the God of the whole earth, and the Lord regards that poor creature as if there were nothing else for Him to observe, bending His ear and His heart to listen to that creature's cry. It is essential that we know that we are speaking to God, and that God is hearing us.

You notice in the Psalms, David says very little about God answering. But David always speaks about God's hearing and asks that He would hear. That He should hear us is quite enough from such a God as He is. If I can get my petition placed in His hand, I am fully satisfied. If I can pour my desire into His ear, all further fear is removed. Your heavenly Father knows that you have need of these things, and you may rest perfectly content. In coming into His presence, you have obeyed His command, and therefore His promise holds good to you. The first thing desired, then, is that the Lord should hear.

But we desire more than that. We desire *that He should accept*. It would be a painful thing to be permitted to speak to a great friend, and then for him to stand austere and stern and say, "I have heard what you have to say. Go your way." We ask not this of God. We come before Him kindly and graciously and ask Him to accept our poor confessions, petitions, supplications, and adorations. If He does but look and smile, if He does but say one word into our soul that implies, "I have accepted your prayer," what a joy it is! To have brought an offering that the Lord has accepted, this is the sweetness and delight of supplication!

There is a third thing that we desire that God gave to Solomon, and that is *an answer*. Solomon asked the Lord to hallow the house, and the Lord did hallow the house. And while there are some things that we must always pray for saying emphatically, "Not as I will, but as thou wilt," yet there are many things that we are encouraged to pray for with importunity, being resolved to have them. There are spiritual and covenant blessings — distinctly promised and evidently essential — that we may ask for without any question, using a sacred importunity and refusing to let the Angel go unless He blesses us. On matters promised by God in His Word we may come again and again, knocking at the Lord's door until He awakes and gives us the loaves that we seek for our hungry and fainting friend (Luke 11:8). Oh, for more holy boldness! Oh, for more assured confidence! We must believe that we have the petitions that we ask of Him. We must ask in faith, without wavering, or we may not expect to receive anything of the Lord.

We long to be heard and answered. We cannot be satisfied to

pray unless we perceive that prayer is effective in the courts above. That is our real goal in prayer.

Our Assurance of Answer to Prayer

Can we have an assurance that God has heard and answered prayer? Solomon had it. The Lord said to him, "I have heard thy prayer and thy supplication, that thou hast made before me." Does the Lord ever say that to us? I think so. Let us consider how He does so.

I think that He says it to us very often *in our usual faith*. I hope that I speak for many readers when I say that we constantly pray in faith. It is habitual with me to expect God to answer me. I go to Him very simply and ask for what I want, and, if I did not receive what I humbly sought, I should be greatly surprised. When I do receive it, I reckon it as a matter of course, for the Lord has promised to answer prayer, and it is certain that He will keep His promise. I am speaking now about the daily mercies, the daily trials, and the ordinary events of life. In these matters God is certain to answer prayer, and our faith hears the voice of God saying, "I have heard thy prayer and thy supplication."

Sometimes you require *strong confidence*. You have need of an extraordinary blessing. You get to a place like that to which Jacob came, when common prayer was not sufficient. When Esau was coming to meet him with an armed force, Jacob must have a night's prayer. He must gather up all his courage at Jabbok; he must wrestle with the Angel and win the divine blessing (Gen. 32). By necessity, at such times a stronger faith is required to assure the soul of the blessing. "According to your faith be it unto you" (Matt. 9:29). If we can trust God, we shall have the thing we seek. Faith is not saying, "I know that I have it," when you really do not have it. That would be telling yourself a lie. A man may say, "Believe that you are sanctified, and you are in a moment sanctified," but you are not. Believing that lie may make you less sanctified than you were before you believed it and ten times more proud, and thus far more under the influence of Satan. To believe that God will sanctify me—and that He is sanctifying me—is a very different thing from believing that I am already sanctified. I believe that

God will supply my needs, but I do not believe that I have the Bank of England in my pocket. Faith is not believing fanatically, but faith is believing the truth. There is a wonderful difference between believing your imaginations and believing what God has distinctly promised. Faith and imagination are two very different things. God keep us from the falsehood of folly and lead us into the truth of wisdom! I will believe anything, however monstrous it may appear, if God says it. I will believe nothing, however desirable, merely because my own imagination desires it. Strong faith often brings with it a conviction within the soul that nothing can shake. It is an assured conviction and yet most reasonable, since it is inspired by the Spirit of God who bears witness only to the truth and not to dreams. To the man's inner consciousness, it is as though he heard the voice of God saying, "I have heard thy prayer and thy supplication."

Sometimes this comes in the form of a *comfortable persuasion*. Have you never ended a prayer when you were in the middle of it and said, "I have been heard"? Have you not felt that you need not continue asking any longer, for you have gained your audience and should instead begin to praise rather than continue to pray? When a man cashes a check at the bank, he moves on to his other business. Oftentimes we are prepared to be a long time in prayer if it should be necessary, yet we feel that we should rather be brief in petition and long in thanksgiving. We rise from our knees with the persuasion, "We need not ask anymore. We have been heard." It is always better to serve God in a pressing practical duty than it is to continue to pray when prayer has no longer any reasonableness in it, seeing that you have already been heard. If God has given you the blessing, why continue to ask for it? "And the LORD said unto Moses, Wherefore criest thou unto me? speak unto the children of Israel, that they go forward" (Ex. 14:15). That going forward was a better thing than praying, now that praying had had its day. There comes a comfortable assurance at times that your prayer is heard, and you go your way rejoicing. This inward persuasion is no fanatical imagining or excitement of the brain but is rather a work of the Holy Spirit that nothing can imitate and only the receiver can understand.

The Lord also gives to His people a *manifest preparation for the blessing*. He prepares them to receive the blessing. Their expectation is raised so that they begin to look for the blessing and make room for it. God never brought you to a well, putting a bucket and rope in your way, without intending to fill that bucket when you let it down. When the thirsty soil has opened all its mouths to drink in the rain of heaven, that rain always comes. When the ears of wheat are ready for the sun to ripen them, the heat of harvest is near. When a man of God so looks for the wind of the Spirit that he spreads the sails of hope, the breeze is sure to blow. It is a lack of preparation that hinders the blessing. "And he did not many mighty works there because of their unbelief" (Matt. 13:58). But when the Lord has given you an evident preparation for the blessing, the blessing is already on the way, and its shadow is resting upon you. In that preparation, the Lord virtually says, "I have heard thy prayer and thy supplication."

Actual observation also cultivates in us a solid confidence that our prayer is succeeding. Sometimes God gives us an assurance that He has heard our prayer when He causes us to look back and observe the past. How He has answered us back then! He changes not; He hears us still. Here I must speak what I know to be true. Throughout life it has been my habit to wait upon God about many things, and especially about extraordinary necessities that have arisen out of the demands of the great institutions committed to me. I shall not detail the stories of the Lord's supplies in answer to prayer, but in very truth, the Lord has heard my prayers as distinctly as if He had rent the heavens and put out His right hand filled with good. The fact that the Lord has heard us in the past speaks in our souls and fills us with the assurance that He will hear us yet again. Memory emphasizes the comforting voice of the Lord, saying, "I have heard your prayer; therefore trust me with all your heart. Have I not always heard your prayers? My beloved one, when did I reject you? In the hour of your distress, have I not delivered you? In the times of your need, have I not supplied you? I have heard your prayer. Go in peace. Weep no more. Let not your soul be troubled. All is well, for I am on the throne of grace, and my face is toward you."

Our Special Application of Prayer

For Solomon, prayer turned in a direction that I want to turn to now. You learn what Solomon's prayer was when you hear how

God fulfilled it. God said to him, "I have hallowed this house which thou hast built, and put my name there for ever, and mine eyes and heart shall be there perpetually." Last night the members of our church held the annual church meeting [February 9, 1887], and we had great joy and thankfulness for all the mercy that God has made to pass before us. I have just completed thirty-three years of ministry here with unbroken blessing. We can say that all these years have passed with no division or strife among us, with nothing but perpetual benedictions from the Lord God of our salvation. Blessed be His name!

Our prayer is again that the Lord Himself would *hallow this house* that we have built. We ask this in no superstitious way. Bricks and cement and irons and stone are nothing to us. The qualities of holiness adhere not to material substances but to hearts and souls and acts. Yet we ask our Lord to hallow this church with His presence still more and more. If His presence departs, Ichabod would be our bitter cry! The glory would indeed have departed. We want our Lord to hallow it by His favorable regard, that when we worship He will accept our worship and hear our prayers and praises. We want Him to hallow it by His working among us in many more conversions. It was a joyous time to me when I saw the inquirer come forward who was number ten thousand, but all is the work of our gracious God. We shall never bring in another true convert unless we have God's presence! O Lord Jesus, we would constrain You saying, "Abide with us." In the breaking of bread, in the ordinance of baptism, in the proclamation of the gospel, and in all our gatherings together, we pray You would hallow our church. We pray it from our inmost souls. You who have found our service to be hallowed to You in days that are past, keep us from failure and famine in the future.

We want that He should hollow our church in this way: *"to put my name there for ever."* "For ever." As long as there shall be any such house—or need of such a house—may His name be here. My venerable predecessor, Dr. Rippon, prayed for a successor whom the Lord would send among the people of his care after his own decease. In a letter that I have seen, I cannot but somehow see myself—as in the glimmer of the firelight he saw the person who would follow him and carry on his work. I think that I may begin to pray after his example, that as long as there shall be the need for a house of God, the name of God may be honored in this church and faithful men may proclaim His salvation in the power of the Holy Ghost. Let the house be wrapped in flames and every ash be blown away by the winds sooner than that any should preach from this pulpit any other gospel than the true gospel.

Solomon prayed also, and God heard him, that *the eye of the Lord might be there.* That was Solomon's prayer, and God greatly improved upon it, for He said that His eye *and His heart* should be there perpetually. Thus, the Lord hears our prayers in a better sense than that in which we offer them. We pray that His eye may be upon us, and He adds, "It shall be so, and with my eye my heart also shall be there." Oh, that the eye of the Lord might be upon this church, to watch over and keep it from all harm! But may His heart also be with us, filling us with His divine life and love and making us to know His inner self! Oh, for the love of God to be shed abroad in our hearts by the Holy Ghost! May we know that God's feelings of affection and delight are toward us! This shall be our joy unspeakable!

*P*rayer is the true gauge of spiritual power. To restrain prayer is a dangerous and deadly tendency. This is a faithful saying: what you are upon your knees, you are really before your God. What the Pharisee and the publican were in prayer was the true criterion of their spiritual state (Luke 18:10–14). You may maintain a decent repute among men, but it is a small matter to be judged of man's judgment, for men see only the surface, while the Lord's eyes pry into the recesses of the soul. If He sees that you are prayerless, He makes small account of your attendance at religious meetings or your loud spiritual words. If you are a man of earnest prayer—and especially if the spirit of prayer is in you so that your heart habitually talks with God— things are right with you. But if this is not the case and your prayers are hindered, there is something in your spiritual system that needs to be ejected or something lacking that needs to be supplied. "Keep thy heart with all diligence; for out of it are the issues of life" (Prov. 4:23); and living prayers are among those issues.

Chapter Ten

Hindrances to Prayer

That your prayers be not hindered—1 Peter 3:7.

TO MERELY BOW THE KNEE in formality or to go through a form of devotion in a careless or half-hearted manner is rather to mock God than to worship Him. It would be dreadful to consider how much of vain repetition and heartless prayer-saying the Lord is wearied with from day to day. Yet I most solemnly remind anyone who does not truly pray that the wrath of God abides on him. He who never seeks for mercy has certainly never found it. Conscience acknowledges it to be a righteous thing with God that He should not give to those who will not ask. It is the smallest thing that can be expected of us that we should humbly ask for the favors we need. If we refuse to do so, it is only right that the door of grace should be closed so long as we refuse to knock.

Prayer is not a hard requirement—it is the natural duty of a creature to its creator, the simplest homage that human need can pay to divine liberality. Those who refuse to render it may well expect that when a time of extreme difficulty comes, they will begin to bemoan their folly and will hear a voice from their insulted God, saying, "Because I have called, and ye refused; I have stretched out my hand, and no man regarded. . . . I also will laugh at your calamity; I will mock when your fear cometh" (Prov. 1:24, 26). If a sinner will not plead the name of Jesus to which the promise of forgiveness is given, if he will not bend his knee in repentance and ask for pardon at the hand of God, no one will wonder that he perishes for his folly. None will be able to accuse the Lord of too great severity when He casts away forever all prayerless souls. For anyone who never prays, I tremble!

To those who do pray, prayer is a most precious thing, for it is the channel by which priceless blessings come to them and the window through which their needs are supplied by a gracious God. To believers, prayer is the great means of soul enrichment— it is the vessel that trades with heaven and comes home from the celestial country laden with treasures of far greater worth than ever Spanish galleon brought from the land of gold. Indeed, to true believers prayer is so invaluable that the danger of hindering it is used by Peter as a motive why—in marriage relationships and household concerns—husbands and wives should behave themselves with great wisdom. He bids the husband "dwell" with his wife "according to knowledge" and render loving honor to her, lest their united prayers should be hindered (1 Pet. 3:7). Anything that hinders prayer must be wrong. If anything regarding the family is injuring our power in prayer, there is an urgent demand for change. Husband and wife should pray together as joint heirs of grace, and any behavior or temper or habit that hinders this is evil.

The text would be most appropriately used to stimulate Christians to diligence in family prayer, and though I shall not use it here, it is not because I undervalue it. I esteem family prayer so highly that no language of mine can adequately express my sense of its value. The house in which there is no family prayer can hardly expect the divine blessing. If the Lord does not cover our habitation with His wings, our family is like a house without a roof. If we do not seek the Lord's guidance, our household is a ship without a pilot. And unless we are guarded by devotion, our family will be a field without a hedge. The distressing behavior of many of the children of Christian parents is mainly due to the neglect or the coldness of family worship. And many a judgment has, I doubt not, fallen upon households because the Lord is not duly honored therein. Eli's sin still brings with it the visitations of a jealous God

(1 Sam. 2:34). The word of Jeremiah bears hard upon prayerless families: "Pour out thy fury . . . upon the families that call not upon thy name" (Jer. 10:25). His mercy visits every house where night and morning prayers are made, but where these are neglected, sin is incurred.

In the good old Puritan times, it was said that if you had walked down a certain street you would have heard in every house the voice of a psalm at a certain hour of the morning and evening, for there was no house then of professed Christians without family prayer. I believe that the bulwark of the Reformation was family worship. Take that away, and you lay England open again to the theory that prayer is most acceptable in the parish church, and so you get into the sacredness of places. Then taking away the priesthood from the father of the family, who should be the priest in his own house, you make a vacancy for a superstitious priesthood. Children who observe that their parents are practically prayerless in the household will grow up indifferent to religion and in many cases will utterly reject Christianity. This is a matter about which the church cannot make an inquisitorial inquiry. It must be left to the good sense and the Christian spirit of the heads of households, and I therefore say all the more strongly that you order things at home that family prayer be not hindered.

At this place, however, I shall use the text for another purpose, applying it to the hindrances that beset private prayer. Our prayer may be hindered thus—first, we may be hindered *from* prayer; second, we may be hindered *in* prayer; and, third, we may be hindered *from our prayers speeding with God*.

Hindered *from* Prayer

To be hindered from prayer may be done *by falling into a generally lax condition in reference to the things of God*. When a man becomes spiritually cold, indifferent, and careless, one of the first things that will suffer will be his prayer life. Prayer is the true gauge of spiritual power. To restrain prayer is a dangerous and deadly tendency. This is a faithful saying: what you are upon your knees, you are really before your God. What the Pharisee and the publican were in prayer was the true criterion of their spiritual state (Luke 18:10–14). You may maintain a decent repute among men, but it is a small matter to be judged of man's judgment, for men see only the surface, while the Lord's eyes pry into the recesses of the soul. If He sees that you are prayerless, He makes small account of your attendance at religious meetings or your loud spiritual words. If you are a man of earnest prayer—and especially if the spirit of prayer is in you so that your heart habitually talks with God—things are right with you. But if this is not the case and your prayers are *hindered*, there is something in your spiritual system that needs to be ejected or something lacking that needs to be supplied. "Keep thy heart with all diligence; for out of it are the issues of life" (Prov. 4:23); and living prayers are among those issues.

Prayers may be hindered *by having too much to do*. In this age, this is a common occurrence. We may have too much business for ourselves. The quiet days of our contented forefathers are gone, and men are not content to earn only as much as is necessary for themselves and families. They must have much more than they can possibly enjoy for themselves or profitably use for others. "Enough is as good as a feast," said the old proverb, but nowadays neither enough nor a feast satisfies men. Many a man who might have been of great service to the church of God becomes useless because he must branch out in some new direction in business that takes up all his spare time. Instead of feeling that his first care should be, "How can I best glorify God?," his all-absorbing object is to "stretch his arms like seas and grasp in all the shore." Thousands, hundreds of thousands, and even millions of dollars cannot silence the greedy horseleech that men have swallowed that continually cries, "Give, give." Many add house to house and field to field, as though they meant to be left alone in the land; alas, that Christians should be infected with the same fever. The rich man in the parable had no time for prayer, for he was busy planning new barns wherein to store his goods, but he had to find time for dying when the Lord said, "This night thy soul shall be required of thee" (Luke 12:20). Beware of "the desire of other things," the disease of riches, the greed insatiable that drives men into the snare of the devil. For if it works in you no other evil, it will do you mischief enough if thereby your prayers are hindered.

We may even have too much to do in God's house, and so

hinder our prayers by being like Martha, who was burdened with much serving (Luke 10:40). I never heard of anyone who was burdened with too much praying. The more we do in this life, the more we should pray. Prayer should balance our service, or rather, it should be the lifeblood of every action and saturate our entire life as the dew of heaven filled Gideon's fleece. We cannot labor too much if prayer is proportionate, but I fear that some of us would do far more if we attempted less and prayed more about it. I even fear that some allow public religious engagements to override private communion with God. They attend too many sermons, too many conferences, too many Bible readings, too many committees, and even too many prayer meetings—all good in their own way, but all acting injuriously when they cramp our private prayer. A friend once said that if the apostles were preaching at her time for private communion with God, she would not forsake her place of prayer to go and hear them. It must be better to be with God than with Peter or Paul. Praying is the end of preaching, and woe to the man who, prizing the means more than the end, allows any other form of service to push his prayers into a corner.

There can be no doubt that prayer also is hindered *by having too little to do*. If you want a thing well done, you must go to the man who has a great deal to do, for he is the man to do it for you. People who have nothing to do generally do it with a great deal of fuss. From morning to night they waste other people's time. Having nothing to do, they are hired by Satan to hinder and injure others. If such people ever do pray, I am sure their indolence must hinder them much. The man who teaches in the slums finds he must cry for help to master those wild young natures. The young woman who has around her a dozen girls whom she longs to bring to the Savior feels it imperative upon her to pray that her girls may be converted to God. The minister whose hands are full of holy toil and whose eyes fail with sacred watching finds he cannot go on without drawing near to his God. If these servants of Jesus had less to do, they would pray less, but holy industry is the nurse of devotion.

I said we might do too much, and I could not balance that truth unless I added that a very large proportion of Christians do too little. God has given them enough wealth to be able to retire from business. They have time upon their hands and even invent ways of spending that time, yet the ignorant require instructing, the sick need visiting, the poor need helping. Should Christians not lay out their abundant leisure in the service of God? I wish that all could say with one of the Lord's saints, "Prayer is my business and praise is my pleasure." But I am sure they never will till the zeal of the Lord's house shall more fully consume them.

Some people hinder their prayers *by a lack of order*. They get up a little too late, chase their work all day, and never overtake it, but are always in a flurry with one duty tripping the heels of another. They have no appointed time for communion with God, and consequently, something or other happens, and prayer is forgotten or so slurred and hurried over that it amounts to little. I wish you would keep a diary of your prayer life next week and see how much time you spend with God out of the twenty-four hours. Much time goes at the table—how much at the mercy seat? Many hours are spent with men—how many with your Maker? You are with your friends on earth—how many minutes are you with your Friend in heaven? You allow yourself space for recreation—what do you set apart for those exercises that in very truth recreate the soul? Other duties should be done, but prayer must not be left undone. It must have its own place and sufficient of it. Care must be taken that our "prayers be not hindered" so that we omit or abridge them.

Hindered *in* Prayer

Here I might go over the same ground as before, remarking that some are hindered while in their prayers by being lax, others by having too much or too little to do, and another class by being in that flurried condition of heart that results from a lack of order. But I need not repeat myself when there is so much to say about being engaged in holy work.

Let us note that some are hindered in prayer *by selecting a poor time and place*. There are times when your letters arrive, when customers call, when people need attention, when workers want orders, and it would be foolish to be going into prayer just then. If you are employed by others, you cannot present to God those hours that belong to your employer; you will be honoring the Lord better by diligence in your calling. There are times that are claimed by the necessities of the household and your lawful calling. These are already the Lord's in another way; let them be used for their own purpose. Never defile one duty with the blood of another. Give to God and prayer those suitable times in which you can reasonably expect to be alone. Of course, you should be in the spirit of supplication all day long, but I am alluding now to times specially devoted to prayer. I say choose a time and a place where you can be free from interruption. A godly lad who had no place at home to pray in went to the stable and climbed up into the hayloft. But very soon someone came up the ladder and interrupted him, so the next time he took care to pull the ladder up after him. It would be well indeed if we could so completely pull the ladder up that neither the devil nor the world could invade our sacred privacy. "But thou, when thou prayest, enter into thy closet, and when thou hast shut thy door, pray to thy Father which is in secret; and thy Father which seeth in secret shall reward thee openly" (Matt. 6:6). Select, then, the best time and place, that your prayers be not hindered.

Worldly cares are frequent and most mischievous hindrances to prayer. A Christian man should be the most careful man in the world, and yet without carefulness. He should be careful not to sin, but as for other matters, he should be "Casting all your care upon him; for he careth for you" (1 Pet. 5:7). To receive everything from God's hands and to trust everything in God's hands is a happy way of living and very helpful to prayer. Has not your Master told you of the ravens and the lilies? Your heavenly Father feeds and clothes them, and will He not clothe you? "Seek ye the kingdom of God; and all these things shall be added unto you" (Luke 12:31). Faith gives peace, and peace leaves the soul clear for prayer. But when care comes in, it confuses the mind and puts the heart away from pleading. A heart clogged with care is like a man trying to swim with heavy clothes. Many a sailor has cut his clothes to pieces because he felt he should sink if he did not get clear of them. I could wish that many Christians would tear themselves away from their excessive worldly engagements, for they have such a mass of care upon them that they scarcely keep their heads above water. Oh, for more grace and less worry! More praying and less hoarding! More intercession and less speculating! As it is, prayers are sadly hindered.

Earthly pleasures, especially of a questionable nature are the worst of hindrances. Some Christians indulge in amusements that I am sure are not consistent with prayer. They resemble flies that plunge into the honey until the sweet sticks to their wings and legs and they cannot fly. How can you come home from frivolity and sin and then look into the face of Jesus? How can the ways of the world be followed and communion with God be maintained? You cannot roll in the mire and then approach with clean garments to the mercy seat. How can you come before the throne of God with petitions when you have just been dishonoring the name of the Most High? O Christian! keep yourself from everything about which you have any doubt as to its rightness or even its expediency, for whatsoever is not of faith is sin and will hinder your prayers.

Prayers may be hindered equally by *worldly sorrow*. Some give way to sorrow so extremely that they cannot even pray. The tears of sorrow dampen the powder of prayer so that a Christian man cannot send his desires heavenward as he should. The sorrow that prevents a man's praying is flat rebellion against the will of God. Our Lord was "exceeding sorrowful, even unto death" (Matt. 26:38), and therefore He prayed. It is right to be sorrowful, but when sorrow is right, it will drive us *to* prayer—not drive us *from* it. When we find our grief at the loss of a loved one or the loss of something precious hinders our prayers, I think we should say to ourselves, "Now I must pray; for it must be wrong for me to not come to my Father for comforting." We deeply sympathize with those who sorrow, but we may not excuse their repining. The "sorrow of the world worketh death" (2 Cor. 7:10) and is unfitting in a child of God. With all your grief, bowed into the very dust of affliction, still be like your Lord and Master and cry, "Nevertheless not as I will, but as thou wilt" (Matt. 26:39). Then your prayers will be helped and not hindered.

There are cases in which prayer is very greatly hindered by a *bad temper*. You cannot speak crossly to workers and family or join in a big fight or in small squabbles and then go and pray with power. I cannot speed in prayer if I feel anger in my heart, and I do not believe that you can. Get up and go and settle the matter before you try to talk with God, for the prayer of angry men makes

God angry. You cannot wrestle with the Covenant Angel while you are under the power of the devil. That was good advice on our Lord's part: "Leave there thy gift before the altar . . . first be reconciled to thy brother" (Matt. 5:24). If that is not done, the sacrifice cannot be accepted, nor do I see how you dare offer it. Offenses will come in this life, but blessed are those who are foremost in removing them. Alas, some cannot do this but will keep a grudge till it rots and fills their whole nature with its vile odors! Surely they cannot expect to be heard in prayer while their unburied enmities pollute their souls. Do endeavor, as much as you can, whenever you are angry, not to sin. It is possible, for it is written, "Be ye angry, and sin not" (Eph. 4:26). A man who has no anger in him is hardly a man, for he who is not angry at sin is not in love with virtue. Anger against injustice is right, but when anger against the person degenerates into wishing him hurt, it is sinful and effectually blows out the fires of prayer. We cannot pray for forgiveness unless we forgive the trespasses of others against us.

Prayers can be hindered—very terribly hindered—in three ways: if we dishonor the Father *to* whom we pray, or the Son *through* whom we pray, or the Holy Ghost *by* whom we pray.

We can dishonor *the Father* by inconsistency of life. If children of God are not obedient to the Father's will, they must not wonder if they find it hard to pray. Something will rise in the throat that will choke their pleading. You cannot pour out your heart acceptably unless you believe in your heavenly Father. If you have distorted thoughts of God, if you have a cold heart toward Him, if you lack a reverence for His name, if you do not believe in that great willing heart that is willing to bless you, your lack of love, faith, and reverence will strangle your prayers. When a man is fully at one with the great Father, when "Abba, Father" is the very spirit of his soul, when a man speaks to God as one in whom he places implicit trust and to whose will he yields himself up perfectly and whose glory is his soul's delight, that man is on excellent ground in prayer, and he will win what he desires of God. If he is not so with God, his prayers will limp most painfully.

Similarly, if we are wrong with *Jesus* through whom we pray, if we are in any measure self-righteous, if we delight in self and forget our Beloved, if we fancy that we can do without the Savior, if we pray like complacent Pharisees, our prayers will be hindered.

If we are not like the Savior; if we do not make Him our example, if we have none of His loving spirit, above all, if we crucify Him afresh and put Him to open shame and if we are ungrateful for the graces we have already received, our prayers will be hindered. You cannot plead in the court if you have quarrelled with your Advocate. If your prayer is not taken in hand by the great Intercessor and offered by Him on your behalf, you will have no heart for the sacred exercise.

So, again, with the *Holy Ghost*. There is never a prayer that God accepts but the Spirit first writes it in our hearts. True prayer is not so much our intercession as the Spirit of God making intercession in us. If we grieve the Spirit, He will not help us to pray. If we attempt to pray for something that is contrary to the Spirit's holy, gracious, loving nature, we cannot expect Him to enable us to pray in contradiction to the mind of God. Take care that you vex not the Spirit of God in any way, especially by shutting your ears to His gentle warnings, His loving calls, His earnest entreaties, His tender admonitions. If you are deaf to the divine Comforter, He will be speechless to you. He will not help you to pray if you will not yield to Him in other matters.

Hindrance in the Speeding of Our Prayers

The Lord will hear any man's prayer who asks for mercy through the mediation of the Lord Jesus. He never despises the cry of the contrite. He is a God ready to hear all who seek reconciliation, but concerning other matters, it is true that God does not hear sinners. A man will grant his child's request, but he does not listen to strangers; he will listen to his friends, but not to enemies. It is not right that the golden key that opens the caskets of heaven should be hung at a rebel's side. Yet more, God does not hear all His children alike, or alike at all times. It is not every believer who is mighty in prayer. Read the Ninety-ninth Psalm and you will find words like these: "Moses and Aaron among his priests, and Samuel among them that call upon his name; they called upon the LORD, and he answered them. . . . they kept his testimonies, and the ordinances that he gave them" (vss. 6–7). He answered *them*— Moses, Aaron, Samuel—for they kept His testimonies. When children of God find that their prayers do not succeed, they should search and discover reasons that their prayers are hindered.

First, there must be *holy living* in a believer if his prayers are greatly to succeed with God. "The effectual fervent prayer of a *righteous man* availeth much" (James 5:16). Note that point—*of a righteous man*. Listen to our Savior: "If ye abide in me, and my words abide in you, ye shall ask what ye will, and it shall be done unto you" (John 15:7). There is an *if* there. If you do not do Christ's will, He will not do your will. This has nothing to do with the law, but it is the gospel rule of Christ's house that obedience should have for its reward power in prayer. Just as you do with your children, you have ways of disciplining the willful and rewarding the obedient. You are in no hurry to grant the requests of your stubborn boy; in fact, you deny him his request; but that other gentle and loving child has only to ask and have. This is correct discipline, and such as God exercises among us. God does not cast off His children for sin and utterly disown them, but He disciplines them in love. And one of His disciplines lies in shutting out their prayers. If we compare prayer to shooting with a bow, you must have clean hands or you cannot shoot, for this bow refuses to bend to hands polluted with unrepented sin. "The desire *of the righteous* shall be granted" (Prov. 10:24), but not the desire of the wicked. First wash in the fountain of atoning grace and have your heart cleansed by the Holy Spirit, for otherwise you cannot succeed in prayer. If anyone should tell me of a man whom God greatly answered in prayer and then inform me that he lived in gross sin, I would not believe it. It is impossible for God to patronize a guilty professor of religion by giving him success in prayer. The blind man whom Jesus healed most truly said, "If any man . . . doeth his will, him he heareth" (John 9:31).

In addition to obedience there must be *faith*. "He that cometh to God must believe that he is, and that he is a rewarder of them that diligently seek him" (Heb. 11:6). "But let him ask in faith, nothing wavering. For he that wavereth is like a wave of the sea, driven with the wind and tossed. For let not that man think that he shall receive anything of the Lord" (James 1:6–7). Faith obtains promises, unbelief goes empty-handed. The Lord may give a blessing to a doubter, but that is more than the promise, and the doubter has no right to expect it. The prayer that avails most with God is the prayer of one who believes that God will hear him and who therefore asks with confidence. In a word, faith is the *bow* of prayer. You must lay hold on the bow or you cannot shoot, and the stronger the bow, the farther you can send the arrow and the more execution you can do with it. Without faith, it is impossible to please God in prayer or in anything else. Faith is the very backbone, sinew, and muscle of intercession.

Third, there must be *holy desires*, or else prayer will be a failure. And those desires must be founded on a promise. If you cannot find that God has promised a blessing, you have no right to ask for it and no reason to expect it. You must bring God's own promises to the mercy seat and you will obtain what you need, but only in that way. Observe, then, that faith is the bow, and strong desire fits to the string the arrow that is to be sent upward. No arrow may be shot toward heaven but that which came down from heaven. Christians take their arrows from God's quiver, and when they shoot them, they do so with this on their lips, "Remember the word unto thy servant, upon which thou hast caused me to hope" (Ps. 119:49). So the successful prayer is the desire of a holy heart, sanctioned by the promise. True prayers are like those carrier pigeons that find their way so well; they cannot fail to go to heaven, for it is from heaven that they came, and they are only going home.

If prayer is to speed, there must be *fervor and importunity*. It is written, "The effectual *fervent* prayer of the righteous man availeth much," not the prayer of one who does not care whether he is answered or not. There must be earnestness, intensity, the pouring out of the heart before God. The arrow must be put on the bowstring, and the bow must be drawn with all our might. The best bow is of no use until you draw it, and if you draw the bow of faith and shoot at the target up there in heaven, you will get what you will. But you *must resolve to have it* with only this boundary— "the will of the Lord be done"—and you will succeed.

A *desire for God's glory* is the white of the target, and if we do not shoot toward that, the arrow will avail nothing. We must earnestly desire what we ask because we believe it will glorify God to give it to us. If we are wholly living for God, our prayers will run side by side with His purposes, and none of them will fall to the ground. "Delight thyself also in the LORD; and he shall give thee the desires of thine heart" (Ps. 37:4).

We must also have a *holy expectancy* or we shall hinder prayer. The man who shoots must look to see where his arrow goes. We must direct our prayer to God and look up. Eyeing the Lord Jesus in all, we must look to succeed through the merits of the Redeemer. "And if we know that he hear us . . . we know that we have the petitions that we desired of him" (1 John 5:15).

Presumption in prayer shoots with the bow of self-confidence—not for God's glory but for the gratification of itself—and therefore it fails. Some have the idea that they may ask what they like of God and are sure to have it. But I would ask them, first, "Who are you?", second, "What is it you are going to ask?", and, third, "What right have you to expect it?" These inquiries must be clearly answered, otherwise prayer may be an insult to God. I wish some Christians who pray about material concerns would be a little more careful as to how they act. When they get into scrapes and messes by extravagance, do they expect God to get them out? Pray by all means, but "owe no man anything" (Rom. 13:8). Daily bread is to be prayed for, but speculations that may involve your ruin or make your fortune are not to be mentioned. If you take to gambling, you may as well give up praying. Straightforward transactions you may pray about, but do not mix up the Lord with your financing.

I am requested to pray that a young man who has lost his house through embezzlement may get another place, but instead of doing so I suggest that he should himself pray to be made honest. Another who is deeply in debt wants me to pray that he may obtain help, but I suggest that he should let his creditors have a dividend while there is anything left. I shall not ask of my God what I would not ask of man. The approach to the mercy seat is holy ground and not to be played with or made to minister to sin. "Ye ask, and receive not, because ye ask amiss, that ye may consume it upon your lusts" (James 4:3). If we walk contrary to the Lord, He will walk contrary to us. I say to every Christian who is in trouble, take the straight path out of it and do the right thing. If it brings you trouble, bear it like a man, and then go to God and say, "Lord, I have, by Your grace, chosen a plain, honest path; now help me," and He will.

May God grant us grace as Christians to walk with Him in the power of His Spirit, resting alone on Jesus. May He make each of us mighty in prayer. A man whom God has taught to pray mightily is one with God's mind and is God's hand moving among the sons of men. When the man acts, God acts with him. He must, however, be careful and watchful, for the Lord is a jealous God and most jealous where He loves most. God grant you to walk humbly with God and to live near to Him, "that your prayers be not hindered."

I suppose it is true for many of us that our cares are manifold. If you are like me, once you become careful, anxious, fretful, you are never able to count your cares, even though you might count the hairs of your head. Cares multiply to those who are care-full. When you are as full of care as you think you can be, you will be sure to find another crop of cares growing up all around you. The indulgence of this habit of anxiety leads to its getting dominion over life till life is not worth living by reason of the care we have about it. Cares and worries are manifold; therefore let your prayers be manifold. Turn everything that is a care into a prayer. Let your cares be the raw material of your prayers. As the alchemist hoped to turn dross into gold, you have the power to actually turn what naturally would have been a care into a spiritual treasure in the form of prayer. Baptize every anxiety into the name of the Father, the Son, and the Holy Ghost, and so make it into a blessing.

Chapter Eleven

Prayer, the Cure for Care

*Be careful for nothing; but in every thing by prayer and suppli-
cation with thanksgiving let your requests be made known unto
God. And the peace of God, which passeth all understanding, shall
keep your hearts and minds through Christ Jesus*—Philippians
4:6–7.

GOD HAS GIVEN US the faculty of fore-
thought. But like all our faculties, it has been perverted and is often
abused. Although it is good for a man to have a holy care and to
pay attention to every item of his life, it is very easy to make his
life into an unholy care and to attempt wrestling from the hand of
God that office of providence that belongs to God exclusively. How
often Martin Luther liked to talk about the birds and the way God
cares for them! When Luther was full of anxieties, he constantly
envied the birds because they led so free and happy a life. He
talked of Dr. Sparrow, Dr. Thrush, and others that used to come
and talk to Dr. Luther and tell him many good things. The truth is
that the birds out in the wild are cared for by God and fare far
better than those that are cared for by man. A little London girl
went into the country and said to her mother, "Look at that poor
little bird; it has no cage!" That did not strike me as being any loss
to the bird. Correspondingly, if you and I were without our cage,

the box of seed, and glass of water, it would not be much of a loss if we were cast adrift into the glorious liberty of a life of humble dependence upon God. It is the cage of carnal trust and the box of seed that we are always laboring to fill that creates the worry of this earthly life. He who has grace to spread his wings and soar away, traveling to the open field of divine trustfulness, may sing all the day.

Here, then, is the teaching of the text: "Be careful for nothing." The word *careful* means *full of care*. The text means that we are to not be anxious, to not be constantly thinking about the needs of this mortal life. Read it again by stretching the word out a little: "Be care-full for nothing." Oh, that God might teach us how to avoid this forbidden evil and to live with that holy carelessness that is the very beauty of the Christian life. Casting all our care on God, we can rejoice in His providential care of us.

"Impossible," says someone. "I cannot stop worrying." Paul's words will help you do the impossible. First, consider *the substitute for care*. Be careful for nothing but be prayerful for everything. The substitute for care is "prayer and supplication." Second, note *the special character of this prayer* that is to become the substitute for anxiety: "In every thing by prayer and supplication with thanksgiving let your requests be made known unto God." And then consider *the sweet effect of this prayer*: "The peace of God, which passeth all understanding, shall keep your hearts and minds through Christ Jesus."

The Substitute for Care

I suppose it is true for many of us that *our cares are manifold*. If you are like me, once you become careful, anxious, fretful, you are never able to count your cares, even though you might count the hairs of your head. Cares multiply to those who are care-full. When you are as full of care as you think you can be, you will be sure to find another crop of cares growing up all around you. The indulgence of this habit of anxiety leads to its getting dominion over life till life is not worth living by reason of the care we have about it. Cares and worries are manifold; therefore let your prayers be manifold. Turn everything that is a care into a prayer . Let your cares be the raw material of your prayers. As the alchemist hoped to turn dross into gold, you have the power to actually turn what naturally would have been a care into a spiritual treasure in the form of prayer. Baptize every anxiety into the name of the Father, the Son, and the Holy Ghost, and so make it into a blessing.

Have you a care you are pursuing? Take heed that it does not get you. Are you desiring to make a financial gain? You should be mindful to not lose more than you gain by your gains. Have no more care to gain than you dare to turn into a prayer. Do not desire to have what you dare not ask God to give you. Measure your desires by a spiritual standard, and you will be kept from anything like covetousness. Cares come to many from their losses; people lose what they have gained. Keep in mind that this is a world where the tendency is to lose. Ebbs follow floods, and winters crush out summer flowers. Do not be surprised if you lose as other people do, but pray about your losses. Go to God with your losses and, instead of fretting, make them an occasion for waiting upon the Lord. Say to God in prayer, "The Lord gave, and the Lord has taken away; blessed be the name of the Lord. Deliver me from ever complaining that You are unfair no matter what You permit me to lose!"

Perhaps you say that your care is not about gaining or losing but about your basic daily bread. Take to heart the promise you have for this care. The Lord has said, "So shalt thou dwell in the land, and verily thou shalt be fed" (Ps. 37:3). The Lord gives you sweet encouragement when He says that He clothes the grass of the field, and shall He not much more clothe you, O ye of little faith? And the Lord Jesus bids you consider the birds of the air, how they neither sow nor gather into barns, and yet your heavenly Father feeds them (Matt. 6:25–33). Go, then, to your God with all your cares. If you have a large family, a slender income, and trouble making ends meet and providing things honest in the sight of all men, you have so many excuses for knocking at God's door, so many more reasons for being often found at the throne of grace. Turn your excuses and reasons to good account. Be bold to call upon God when necessities press upon you. Instead of anxiety and worry, turn your care into a reason for renewed prayerfulness.

"Ah," says one, "but I am perplexed! I am involved in a situation in which I do not know what to do." You should certainly pray when you cannot tell whether it is the right-hand road or the left-hand or straight on or whether you should go back. Indeed, when you are in such a fog that you cannot see the next light, then is the time that you must pray. The road will clear before you very suddenly. I have often found this true in my life, and I confess that when I have trusted in myself, I have been a gigantic fool. But when I have trusted in God, He has led me straight on in the right way, and there has been no mistake about it. I believe that God's children often make greater blunders over simple things than they do over more difficult matters. When the Gibeonites came to Israel with their old shoes and showed the bread that was moldy, they said they took the bread fresh out of their ovens. The children of Israel thought, "This is a clear case. These men are strangers, having come from a far country, and we may make a covenant with them." The Israelites were certain that the evidence of their eyes proved that these were not Canaanites, so they did not consult God. Such a compromise was a trouble for God's people ever afterward. If in everything we would go to God in prayer, our perplexities would lead us into no more mistakes than our simplicities, and in simple things and difficult things we would be guided by the Most High.

Perhaps you say, "But I am thinking about the future." Are you? Let me ask you what you have to do with the future? Do you know what a day will bring? You worry about what will become of you when you are old, but are you sure that you ever will be old? I know a Christian woman who worried herself about how she would get buried. That question never troubled me, and there are many other matters that need not worry us. You can always find a stick with which to beat a dog, and if you want a care, you can always find a care with which to beat your soul; but that is a poor occupation for anyone. Instead of doing that, turn everything that might be a subject of care into a subject of prayer. It will not be long before it becomes a holy habit. Cross out the word *care* and write in its place the word *prayer*. Then, though your cares are manifold, your prayers will also be manifold.

Note next that *undue care is an intrusion into God's province.* It is making yourself the father of the household instead of being a child. It is making yourself the master instead of being a servant for whom the master provides. If, instead of doing that, you turn care into prayer, there is no intrusion, for you may come to God in prayer without being charged with presumption. God invites you to pray. By His servant, He commands you "in every thing by prayer and supplication with thanksgiving let your request be made known unto God."

Furthermore, *cares are of no use to us, and they cause us great damage.* If you were to worry as long as you wished, you could not make yourself an inch taller. So the Savior tells us, and He asks, if care fails in such little things, what can care do in the higher matters of providence? It cannot do anything. A farmer stood in his fields and said, "I do not know what will happen to us. The wheat will be destroyed if this rain keeps on. We shall not have any harvest at all unless we have some fine weather." He walked up and down, wringing his hands and fretting, making his whole household miserable. But he did not produce one single gleam of sunlight by all his worrying. He could not puff any of the clouds away with all his petulant speech, nor could he stop a drop of rain with all his murmurings.

Why allow care to keep gnawing at your own heart when you can get nothing by it? Besides, it weakens our power to help ourselves, and especially our power to glorify God. A care-full heart hinders us from seeing anything clearly. It is like taking a telescope, breathing on it with the hot breath of our anxiety, putting it to our eye, and then saying that we cannot see anything but clouds. Of course we cannot, and we never shall as long as we breathe upon it. If we were calm, quiet, self-possessed, we should do the right thing. We should be, as we say, "all there" in the time of difficulty. That man may expect to have presence of mind who has the presence of God. If we forget to pray, do we wonder that we are all in a worry and do the first thing that occurs to us—which is generally the worst thing—instead of waiting till we see what should be done and then trustfully and believingly doing it as in the sight of God? Care is harmful. But if you only turn this care into prayer, every care will be a benefit to you.

Prayer is wonderful material for building up the spiritual fabric. We are personally edified by prayer. We grow in grace by prayer. And if we will but come to God every moment with petitions, we shall be growing Christians. I said to someone, "Pray for me. It is a time of need." She replied, "I have done nothing else since I woke." I have made the same request of several others, and they have said that they have been praying for me. I felt so glad, not only for my own sake who had received benefit from their prayers but also for their sakes, because they are sure to grow thereby. When little birds keep flapping their wings, they are learning to fly. The muscles will get stronger, and the birds will leave the nest before long. So to the attempting to pray, the groaning, the sighing, the crying of a prayerful spirit, is itself a blessing. Break off, then, this damaging habit of care and take to this enriching habit of prayer. You will make a double gain by avoiding a loss and by getting that which will really benefit both you and others.

Then, again, *cares are the result of forgetfulness of Christ's closeness to us.* Notice how the context runs. Philippians 4:5 ends with "The Lord is at hand." Our text continues: "Be careful for nothing." The Lord Jesus Christ has promised to come again, and He may come at any moment. Thus, Paul writes, "The Lord is at hand. Be careful for nothing; but in every thing by prayer and supplication with thanksgiving let your requests be made known unto God." If we could but stand on this earth as upon a mere shadow and live as those who will soon be done with this poor transient life! If we held every earthly thing with a very loose hand, we would not be caring and worrying and fretting, but we would be praying, for thus we grasp the real, the substantial, and plant our feet upon the invisible—which is, after all, the eternal! Let the text drop into your heart as a pebble falls into a mountain lake, and as it enters, let it make rings of comfort upon the very surface of your soul.

The Special Character of This Prayer

First, it is *a prayer that deals with everything.* "In *every thing* let your requests be made known unto God." You may pray about the smallest thing and the greatest thing. You not only may pray for the Holy Spirit, but you may pray for a new pair of boots. You may go to God about the bread you eat, the water you drink, the clothing you wear, and pray to Him about everything. Draw no line that limits the care of God. Oh, that we might live in God as to the whole of our being, for our being is such that we cannot divide it! Our body, soul, and spirit are one, and while we have necessities that arise out of the condition of our bodies, we must bring our bodily necessities before God in prayer. You will find that the great God will hear you in these matters. Never say that daily necessities are too little for Him to notice; everything is little in comparison with Him. When I think of what a great God He is, it seems to me that this poor little world of ours is just one insignificant grain of sand on the seashore of the universe and not worth any notice at all. If God condescends to consider this world, He may as well stoop a little lower and consider us. And He does, for He says, "Even the very hairs of your head are all numbered" (Luke 12:7). Therefore, in everything let your requests be made known to God.

The kind of prayer that saves us from care is *prayer that is repeated*: "In every thing by prayer and supplication." If the Lord does not answer you the first time, be very grateful that you have a good reason for praying again. If He does not grant your request the second time, believe that He loves you so much that He wants to hear your voice again. If He keeps you waiting till you have gone to Him seven times, say to yourself, "Now I know that I worship the God of Elijah, for Elijah's God let him go again seven times before the blessing was given." Count it an honor to be permitted to wrestle with the Angel. This is the way God makes His princes. Jacob would never have been Israel if he had obtained the blessing from the Angel at the first asking. When Jacob had to keep on wrestling till he prevailed, he became a prince with God. The prayer that kills care is prayer that perseveres.

Next, it is *intelligent prayer*: "Let your requests be made known unto God." If you go to God and simply repeat a certain formula, it will be only a mouthful of words. What does God care about that kind of praying? "Let your requests be made known unto God"—that is true prayer. God does know what your requests are, but you are to pray to Him as if He did not know. You are to make known your requests—not because the Lord does not know, but perhaps because you do not know—and when you have made your requests known to Him, you will more clearly have made them known to yourself. When you have asked intelligently, knowing what you have asked and why you have asked it, you will perhaps stop and say to yourself, "No, I must not, after all, make that request." Sometimes, when you have gone on praying for what God does not give you, it may be that there will steal over your mind the conviction that you are not on the right track. That result of your prayer will in itself do you good and be a blessing to you.

But you are to pray, making your requests known to God. In plain English this means *to say what you want*, for this is true prayer. Get alone and tell the Lord what you want, pouring out your heart before Him. Do not imagine that God requires any fine religious language. Pray for what you want in the same words you tell your mother or your dearest friend what your need is. Go to God in that manner, for that is the real prayer, and that prayer will drive away your care.

The kind of prayer that brings freedom from care is *communion with God*. If you have not spoken to God, you have not really prayed. A little child was known to go and put a letter down the grating of a drain, and, of course, there was never any reply to the letter. If the letter is not put into the mailbox, it is no surprise it never makes it to the person to whom it is addressed. Similarly, prayer is real communication with God. You must "believe that he is, and that he is a rewarder of them that diligently seek him" (Heb. 11:6) or else you cannot pray. God must be a reality to you, a living reality. You must believe that He does hear prayer, and then you must speak with Him and believe that you have the petition that you ask of Him, and so you shall have it. He has never failed to honor believing prayer. He may keep you waiting for a while, but delays are not denials. He has often answered a prayer that asked for silver by giving gold. He may have denied earthly treasure, but He has given heavenly riches of ten thousand times the worth, and the suppliant has been more than satisfied with the exchange. "Let your requests be made known unto God." I know what you do when you are in trouble: you run to your friend, but your friend does not always want to hear about your troubles. But if you go to your God, He will never give you the cold shoulder. He will never say that you come too often. On the contrary, He will even chide you because you do not come to Him often enough.

There is one word that I have left for my last observation on this point: "By prayer and supplication *with thanksgiving* let your requests be made known unto God." Now what does that mean? It means that the kind of prayer that kills care is *a prayer that asks cheerfully, joyfully, thankfully*. "Lord, I am poor. Let me bless You for my poverty, and then, O Lord, will You not supply all my needs?" That is the way to pray. "Lord, I am ill. I bless You for this affliction, for I am sure that it means some good thing to me. Now be pleased to heal me, I beseech You!" "Lord, I am in a great trouble. But I praise You for the trouble, for I know that it contains a blessing though the envelope is black-edged. Lord, help me through my trouble!" That is the kind of prayer that kills care—"supplication with thanksgiving." Mix these two things, rub them well together, and they will make a blessed cure for care. May the Lord teach us to practice this holy art.

The Sweet Effect of This Prayer

"And the peace of God, which passeth all understanding, shall keep your hearts and minds through Christ Jesus." If you can pray in this fashion—instead of indulging evil anxiety—the result will be that *an unusual peace* will steal over your heart and mind. I say unusual, for it is "the peace of God." What is God's peace? It is the unruffled serenity of the infinitely happy God, the eternal composure of the absolutely well-contented God. This shall possess your heart and mind. Notice how Paul describes it: "the peace of God, which passeth all understanding." Other people will not understand how you can be so quiet and full of peace. What is more, you will not be able to tell them, for if it surpasses all understanding, it certainly passes all expression. And what is even more wonderful—you will not understand it yourself.

It will be such a peace that it will be *unfathomable and immeasurable to you.* When one of the martyrs was about to burn for Christ, he said to the judge who was giving orders to fire the pile, "Will you come and lay your hand on my heart?" The judge did so. "Does it beat fast?" inquired the martyr. "Do I show any signs of fear?" "No," said the judge. "Now lay your hand on your own heart and see whether you are not more excited than I am." Think of that man of God who, on the morning he was to be burned, was so soundly asleep that they had to shake him to wake him. He had to get up to be burned, and yet knowing that it was to be so, he had such confidence in God that he slept sweetly. This is "the peace of God, which passeth all understanding." During the Diocletian persecutions when the Christian martyrs came into the amphitheater to be torn by wild beasts or were set in a red-hot iron chair or smeared with honey to be stung to death by wasps and bees, they never flinched. Think of that brave man who was put on a gridiron to be roasted to death and said to his persecutors, "You have done me on one side; now turn me over to the other." Why this peace under such circumstances? It was "the peace of God, which passeth all understanding." After there had been a great storm, the Master stood up in the prow of the vessel and said to the winds, "Peace, be still," and a great calm followed (Mark 4:39). Have you ever felt this calm? You do feel it if you have learned this sacred art of making your requests known to God in everything, and the peace of God which passes all understanding is keeping your hearts and minds through Jesus Christ.

This blessed peace *is a guardian peace* that keeps our hearts and minds. The Greek word implies a garrison. Is it not odd that a military term is used here and that it describes a peace that acts as a guard to the heart and to the mind? It is the peace of God that is to protect the child of God—a strange but beautiful figure. Though it seems like a weakness, peace is the essence of strength, and while it guards, it also feeds us and supplies all our needs.

It is also *a peace that links us to Jesus*: "The peace of God which passeth all understanding, shall keep your hearts and minds"—that is, your affections and your thoughts, your desires and your intellect, your heart so that it shall not fear, your mind so that it shall not know any kind of perplexity—through Jesus Christ. It is all "through Christ Jesus," and therefore it is double sweet and precious to us.

The blessed habit of going to God in prayer and casting all our care upon Him helps us to live most joyfully even in this life. If you have a living God, and you have real fellowship with Him—constantly, as a habit, living beneath the shadow of the wings of the Almighty—then you shall enjoy a peace that shall make others wonder and make you marvel, too, even "the peace of God, which passeth all understanding." God grant it to you for Christ's sake!

The prayers the Lord accepts are not the chantings of functionaries, the litanies of priests, or the devout tones of an organ—they must be the prayers of the saints. In the believer's life, character, and soul, the sweetness lies. The acceptance comes not unless they are the prayers of the saints. And who are the saints? They are those whom the Lord has made holy by the power of His Spirit, whose nature He has purified, whom He has washed in the precious blood of Jesus and so sanctified unto Himself, whom He has filled with His Spirit and so set apart to His worship. They love Him, praise Him, bow before Him with solemn awe, lift their whole souls up in adoring love to Him. Their thoughts, desires, longings, confessions, pleadings, and praises are sweet to God. This is music to Him, perfume to His heart, delight to His Infinite mind, and pleasant to His sacred spirit, for "God is Spirit: and they that worship him must worship him in spirit and in truth" (John 4:24). After no other fashion is a spiritual God to be worshipped.

Chapter Twelve

Golden Vials Full of Odors

Golden vials full of odours, which are the prayers of saints—
Revelation 5:8.

THE VISION OF THE FIFTH CHAPTER of Revelation is very remarkable. We do not intend to go into all the details of it. No doubt it is a vision referring to some special occasion, but at the same time we may regard it as descriptive of the usual worship that is offered before the throne of God and the Lamb. We have sometimes seen in European galleries a medieval painting representing the assembly of the great council of the ancient German Empire. There is the emperor surrounded by the various kings, princes, electors, dukes, and counts. Yonder are the knights of the Golden Fleece with the bishops and the cardinals, the barons, knights, and burghers of various degrees making up a marvelous spectacle of pomp and pageantry. We might discover the one particular occasion that the picture represented, but even without such investigation the painting is instructive. We know that it represents the Diet as it might stand for all time. And so in the great assembly of heaven, the outline that the seer of Patmos gives us here may accurately be referred to as one particular event, but it will suffice for us to believe that it represents in general the homage that is rendered at the throne of the Eternal.

In considering the brilliant scene before us, note carefully that the worship described is not confined to the occupants of heaven's immediate courts. From the thirteenth verse we are taught that the scene represents the adoration of the Lamb by the entire universe: "Every creature which is in heaven, and on the earth, and under the earth, and such as are in the sea, and all that are in them, heard I saying, Blessing and honour, and glory, and power, be unto him that sitteth upon the throne, and unto the Lamb for ever and ever." The presence angels lead the strain, the saints made perfect join the rapturous hallelujah, and then ten thousand times ten thousand angels swell the growing strain. Meanwhile, from every starry orb comes up its note of worship, the firmament rings with music. Earth from afar has heard the sound and wakens all her life to take its part in the harmony—the birds of the air, the fish of the sea, the songsters of the wood, and the monsters of the deep render with zeal their tribute of grateful praise. It is not the inner circle alone who thus resounds Jehovah's praise, but widening and widening, the praise encompasses all space and fills immensity. Not heaven alone, but all creation yields the Lord His praise.

Let us by faith pass into the inner circle, draw near to the throne, and gaze upon the golden vials full of odors. The Greek idea for *golden vials* is of a vessel that is both shallow and broad. A better rendering would be *golden bowls* or *golden goblets full of odor* or *full of incense, which are the prayers of saints*. The idea is that each one of the twenty-four elders bears an open bowl or censer filled with smoking incense that pours forth a sweet perfume before the Lord, and this is the symbol of the supplications of the people of God.

Leaving the figure, the thoughts we draw from the text are these. *The prayers of God's people are sweet as incense to Him.* Second, *their blended prayers are particularly acceptable in His sight.* And, therefore, *let us unite our supplications with the general prayer.*

Believers' Prayers Are as Sweet Incense

That prayer is pleasing to God is not due to any natural excellence or merit that believers possess in themselves and by themselves. Far from it. In the best prayer that was ever offered by the holiest man that ever lived there was enough of imperfection and sin to render it a polluted thing if the Lord had looked upon it by itself. When we approach nearest to the throne of grace, we still fall very far short of being where and what we ought to be. The sins of our holy things are alone enough to condemn us. We often come before God in prayer unfit to pray and spoil the action in the very outset by unpreparedness of heart. At other times, when we are in the midst of devotion and are being upborne upon the wings of zeal, pride intrudes and congratulates us upon the excellence of our worship. Alas, one dash of that Pharisaic spirit mars all of our devotion! At other times, just as our prayer is closing, we are assailed with suspicions as to the faithfulness of God, doubts as to the success of our pleas, or else some other unhallowed thought pollutes the sacrifice. How hard it is to begin, continue, and end a prayer in the Spirit! No, the prayers of the saints by themselves considered would rather be an offense to divine holiness than a sweet fragrance to God. Our consolation lies in this that our beloved intercessor who stands before God for us, even Christ Jesus, possesses such an abundance of precious merit that He puts fragrance into our supplications and imparts a delicious odor to our prayers. He makes our intercessions to be through His merit what they could not have been without it—acceptable before the Majesty of heaven.

It was the early church father Ambrose who used a wonderful illustration concerning believers' prayers. He said we are like little children who run into the garden to gather flowers to please their father, but we are so ignorant and childish that we pluck as many weeds as flowers, and some of them are very noxious. We carry this strange mixture in our hands, thinking that it is acceptable to him. The mother meets the child at the door and says, "Little one, you don't know what you have gathered." She unbinds the mixture and takes from it all the weeds, leaving only the sweet flowers, and then she takes other flowers sweeter than those the child plucked and inserts them instead of the weeds. Then she puts the perfect posy into the child's hand, and he runs with it to his father. Jesus Christ in more than motherly tenderness thus deals with our supplications. If we could see one of our prayers after Christ Jesus has amended it, we would hardly recognize it. Jesus has such skill that even our good flowers grow fairer in His hand. We clumsily tie them into a bundle, but He arranges them into a fair bouquet, where each beauty enhances the charm of its neighbor. If I could see my prayer after the Lord has prayed it, I would discover so much missing and so much there that was none of mine that I am sure its fullest acceptance with God would not cause me a moment's pride. It would rather make me blush with grateful humility before Him whose boundless sweetness lent to me and my poor prayer a sweetness not my own. So then, though the prayers of God's saint are as precious incense, they would never be a sweeter fragrance to God were it not that they are accepted in the Beloved.

Note that true, acceptable intercession must be composed of the prayers *of saints*. "Golden goblets full of the prayers of the saints." Nothing is here said of the prayers of church officials or priest. It is thought by some churches most important that there should be kept up a daily repetition of certain words and sounds. This is done not by persons selected for their eminent spirituality or prevalence in prayer but by officials whose appointment is arranged on very different principles. Then, having certain words before them, they have nothing to do but with appointed bowings to go through them, and in going through them they believe they have offered to God acceptable prayer. Based on this type of praying, I have always been expecting to hear that before long praying to God would come to be managed by machinery. The fact is, vocal prayers are nothing in themselves—whether they be said or sung, read or intoned. It is the heart that alone prays acceptably.

If God would be adored with glittering blue, look at the azure of the sky or the deep blue of the sea. If He would be worshipped with lamps and candles, behold the star, and sun, and moon. If He would be reverenced with music, hark how the thunder rolls like drums in His awful march. Is the Infinite mind to be worshipped by vain shows? O you sons of earth, will you thus worship Him that rides on the heavens, before whom you all are but as grasshoppers? The prayers the Lord accepts are not the chantings of functionaries, the litanies of priests, or the devout tones of an organ—they must be the prayers of the saints. In the believer's life, character, and soul, the sweetness lies. The acceptance comes not unless they are the prayers of the saints. And who are the saints? They are those whom the Lord has made holy by the power of His Spirit, whose nature He has purified, whom He has washed in the precious blood of Jesus and so sanctified unto Himself, whom He has filled with His Spirit and so set apart to His worship. They love Him, praise Him, bow before Him with solemn awe, lift their whole souls up in adoring love to Him. Their thoughts, desires, longings, confessions, pleadings, and praises are sweet to God. This is music to Him, perfume to His heart, delight to His Infinite mind, and pleasant to His sacred spirit, for "God is Spirit: and they that worship him must worship him in spirit and in truth" (John 4:24). After no other fashion is a spiritual God to be worshipped.

In the matter of intercession, one of the most important things is the character of the person. If I live in constant sin and then say, "Our Father, which art in heaven," surely I might feel His hand closing my mouth and hear Him say, "How can you hallow My name when you constantly defile it? How can you say, 'Thy kingdom come,' when you will not submit to My rule? How dare you mutter out before Me the words, 'Thy will be done in earth, as it is in heaven,' when you rebel against My will?" Such prayers are an insult to heaven instead of sweet perfume offered before the Most High. Even where the man who presents intercessory prayer is a child of God, unless he maintains his character as a saint in the power of God's Spirit, he will not preserve the prevalence of his prayers. Though our heavenly Father does not hear our prayers because of any merit in us, yet it is written, "If ye abide in me, and my words abide in you, ye shall ask what ye will, and it shall be done unto you" (John 15:7).

If we turn aside from the Lord's commands, we shall lose power in prayer, and our petitions will cease to bring down answers of peace. It is certain there is nothing that so weakens prayer as sin and that to be a man like Elijah, who can prevail with God upon Carmel, you must walk in the Lord's ways—for if you walk contrary to Him, He will walk contrary to you. In the golden bowls, the sweet incense is the prayers not of hypocrites or formalists but of saints. We must, by the Spirit's power, maintain the saintly character; we must walk apart from worldliness and covetousness; we must put aside uncleanness, anger, wrath, and every evil thing or else we shall not be able to present unto the Lord such sweet fragrances as His soul delights in.

These prayers must be *compounded of precious graces*. They are compared to incense, and the incense used in the temple was made up of diverse sweet spices, compounded "according to the work of the apothecary" (Ex. 37:29). Stacte and onycha and galbanum were mixed with pure frankincense, tempered together, and beaten fine. In prayer, that which is sweet to God is not the words used, though they ought to be appropriate; but the sweetness lies not in anything perceptible to the outward senses but in the secret qualities comparable to the essence and aroma of sweet spices. In the incense there lies a subtle and almost spiritual essence that is drawn from it by the burning coals that causes the latent sweetness to spread itself abroad till all around confess its power. So it is in prayer. Our prayers may be very beautiful in appearance and might appear to be the very paragon of devotion, but unless there is a secret spiritual force in them, they are vain things. Faith must be a part of the fragrance of prayer. I am not able to tell when I hear a person pray whether he prays in faith or not, but God perceives the faith or the absence of it, and the prayer is received or rejected as the case may be.

So, too, in prayer there must be the true frankincense of love. How can I pray as a child to a father whom I do not love? If my heart is cold toward God, my prayer will be frozen to death. There is need, moreover, of the grace of humility to be mixed with the other ingredients, for he who does not pray humbly will be no more justified than the Pharisee. There was much of this precious spice in the publican's prayer, when he dared not lift so much as his eyes toward heaven but smote upon his breast, saying, "God be merciful to me a sinner" (Luke 18:13). Much of this should be added to every prayer.

But I cannot tell you what all the separate spices should be that are needed to make up the incense of an acceptable prayer. Only let me remind you that the incense of the temple was mingled "according to the art of apothecary." Let us bless God that the Holy Ghost is the believer's apothecary. He alone knows the proper quantity of each ingredient—how much of faith, how much of love, how much of repentance, how much of humility there should be in every supplication. He helps each believer's weaknesses and makes for us a mixture of all choice graces, so that when we pray, our pleadings are accepted as sweet incense. They are acceptable because they contain a harmonious amalgamation of all the things that are sweet to the Lord God.

Let us also observe that this incense, to be accepted before God, *must burn*. It might be the best incense in the world, well compounded and put into the golden goblets, but it was never accepted by God until it was set on blaze. Live coals must be taken from off the altar and applied to the spices, and then the clouds of the sweet smoke begin to rise up toward heaven. This is where many men's prayers fail. They are correct but cold, excellent but lifeless. They lack life, vigor, earnestness, and fire. Some make up for this deficiency by noise and wildfire, but they will not do. The Holy Spirit alone can give us true passion.

I confess that I have too often prayed in public and not used the holy violence that wins with heaven. In our prayer meetings I have heard excellent supplications that have failed only in this— the living fire had never touched them. How often in the family we go through the usual petitions, praying for ourselves and for the church and for the lost, and so on, and then we go our way. We knelt down mechanically, and we continued there mechanically, and we rose up mechanically. And though the prayer was real, yet I fear there was not more heart in it than if we had read it from a book.

Remember well the truth that no prayer is of any use unless holy fire consumes it. We must have the live coals. I have heard prayers made up of broken, fragmentary, ill-assorted sentences, but the man who presented them has been all alive, and I have blessed God and felt I could say, "Amen, amen, the Lord hear that brother's petition." Have you not gone to prayer and felt, "I have only one thing upon my mind, but oh, how heavily that weighs upon me! I could not construct an elaborate prayer if it were to save my life, for I am so distressed about that one thing"? But that one petition has poured forth from you with all your soul, and you know you have been heard concerning it. The Lord teach us to pray in earnest. May He send His own fire and the heavenly flame of His Spirit, the spirit of grace and supplication, that saints may know how to pray, for we must have the fire with the incense.

Then the fire being with the incense, it was necessary for acceptance that *it should ascend*. If the wind had blown the smoke of the incense downward, scattering it to the right and to the left, it would have been an ill omen. But the incense was accepted with God as it went straight up in the air, mounting till it seemed to join the clouds and lose itself. And so our intercessions—when they are sweet to God—go straight up to Him. Do your prayers always do that? Have you never prayed thinking, "Well, that was a very nice expression that I have used. Spiritual friends will be able to join in and will think, *What a spiritual man he is to pray as he is doing now.*" Ah, the smoke is blowing down, you see, blowing away toward man's nostrils, and not toward God. So much waste—and only waste! The prayer that God accepts is offered to Him alone. He who presents it cares not one atom who likes it or who does not like it. He is talking with his God, pleading with the Majesty unseen. He is very careless of the criticism of others. His only desire is to please the Lord. The prayers of the churches will never be accepted before God until they go straight up to Him, only having respect to Him who is invisible.

The question returns, why are the prayers of saints so sweet to God? We reply, partly because they are the works of the Spirit of God. There is no acceptable prayer in the world but that which the Spirit of God has inspired. The Holy Ghost knows what the mind of God is, and He writes it upon the minds of God's people, "he maketh intercession for the saints according to the will of God" (Rom. 8:27). When God sees His own will reflected in the bosoms of His own children, He cannot but accept the work of His own Spirit.

The prayers of His saints are acceptable with Him also because they are the pleadings of His Son. The saints are members of Christ's body, and as they plead, Christ pleads in them. The very strength of their pleading lies in this—that they urge His merits— and the Lord delights to be reminded of His Son's excellencies. It is a theme that His soul delights in. You may ring that bell as long as you will. The Father will never weary of it. Tell Him what His Son has done. Remind Him of Gethsemane. Bring before the Father's mind the cross of Calvary. Tell Him of His promise to His Son that He shall see His seed and have a full reward. You cannot by any possibility displease God by dwelling upon this topic. Hold Him with the resolution of a Jacob, and say, "I will not let You go unless You bless me, for I plead the name and merit of Your only begotten Son." Everything about Christ is sweet to God, and because believers' prayers are full of Christ, they are sweet to God.

The prayers of the saints are sweet to God because they honor

Him, and this they do in many ways. First, they assert His existence. In prayer the people of God declare better than they could by any other means their sure belief that God is, for should we pray to One who has no existence? Our prayer to God, therefore, is our continual assertion that "The Lord He is God." Our asking for and expecting special mercies is a declaration of our belief in a living God, a conscious God, an acting God, a God who is near at hand listening to human voices and able to fulfill human desires. This, then, is very agreeable to God that we should believe and testify that He is and that He is the rewarder of them that diligently seek Him (Heb. 11:6).

What if I were to say that prayer is in itself essentially a doxology? It is an utterance of glory to God in His attributes. Do I ask Him to bless me? Then I adore His power, for I believe He can. Do I ask Him to bless me? Then I adore His mercy, for I trust and hope He will. Do I ask Him to bless me because of such and such a promise? Then I adore His faithfulness, for I evidently believe that He is truthful and will do as He has said. Do I ask Him to bless me not according to my request but according to His own wisdom? Then I adore His wisdom; I am evidently believing in His prudence and judgment. When I say to Him, "Not my will but thine be done," I am adoring His sovereignty. When I confess that I deserve to suffer beneath His hand, I reverence His justice. When I acknowledge that He always does right, I adore His holiness. When I humbly say, "Nevertheless, deal graciously with me and blot out my transgressions," I am reverencing His grace. We do not wonder, therefore, that through Jesus Christ the prayers of the saints should be precious to God, since they are an eminently practical homage to the Supreme.

Perhaps the best reason we can ever give that God loves to hear us pray is one that comes home to our own hearts. You love to hear your own little children's talk. You know very well when your little girl needs a new dress and your little boy needs schoolbooks, but you like them to feel their needs and to recognize that their needs are supplied by their father. And you love to hear them express their desires. Sometimes you will stop a bit and say, "Why should I give you these?" You set them to pleading because you like to hear their little voices and to have them put their little arms around your neck and overcome you with kisses. You let them believe that they master you with their pretty reasonings and fond embraces, and it is pleasant to you as well as to them. Our heavenly Father is far above us, and yet He bids us learn His character from our own feelings as parents. "If ye then, being evil, know how to give good gifts unto your children: how much more shall your heavenly Father give the Holy Spirit to them that ask him?" (Luke 11:13). The Lord declares that He deals with us as with children. And though the next word is, "For what son is he whom the father chasteneth not?" (Heb. 12:7), I do not believe that God's likeness to a father is limited to His chastening. The text cannot be so cross and crabbed as that. There is a likeness to a father in God's hearing our cries. God loves communion with His people. The Lord loves to have the hearts of His children talk to Him. He delights to hear them speak out their needs and desires before Him and order their case with arguments and prevail with them. Oh, then never slack in your pleadings, which are pleasant to God as fragrant incense!

Blended Prayers Are Particularly Acceptable

"The prayers of saints." The prayers of *a saint* are sweet, but the prayers of *saints* are sweeter. United prayers possess the power of harmony. In music there is melody in any distinct note, but we have all recognized a peculiar charm in harmony. Now the prayers of one saint are to God melody, but the intercessions of many are harmony, and to God there is much that is pleasing in the harmony of His people's prayers.

No two children of God pray exactly alike. There is a difference of tone. If taught of God, each child will pray graciously, but there will be in one prayer what there is not in another. Even though all the fruits of the garden are luscious, each one has its own special flavor. All the bells may be of silver, and yet each one will have its own tone. Some brethren when they pray dwell very tenderly upon the dishonor done to God by sin. They pray as if they would break their hearts and weep at every other sentence. "O God, the idols are placed on Your throne. Jesus is dishonored, the law is broken, the gospel is despised." Such loving contrition for the sin of others wails itself out in soft, low notes of magic power. Listen to others, and you will find their prayers pitched upon quite another key.

The brother prays with full assurance that God's kingdom is established upon the mountains, where its foundation can never be removed. Though the heathen rage and the people imagine a vain thing, yet surely God's kingdom and purpose will stand, and God will do all His pleasure. As you hear such petitioning—bold and clear like the sound of a trumpet—you feel that the voice of faith is both musical and prevalent. The man has no doubt as to God's triumphing, and he prays in that spirit.

If these varying tones are melted into one, what masterly harmony they make! Therefore, the Lord promises great things when two of us agree as touching anything concerning His kingdom (Matt. 18:19). But now comes in a third petitioner, and his tone differs from the other two. The same spirit of prayer is in him, but his voice varies. He prays in this way. Bowed down with a sense of awe in the presence of God, the God of all the earth, he seems to speak, measuring out each word, and he cries, "O God, shall not the nations fear You? Such a One as You are, shall they not tremble in Your presence? Will You not be king to them, O Thou Creator and Preserver of all things?" Like the cherubim, he veils his face in the presence of the excellent glory, and your soul by his prayer is solemnly ushered into the presence of God and laid prostrate there. But mark yet this fourth man, whose prayer is of another mold. He is familiar with the Lord and seems to have merged his sense of the sublime in that of the condescending, speaking somewhat like this: "O Lord, my Father, You love the sons of men, will You not come and meet Your prodigal sons who are coming back to You? Have You not given Jesus Christ to be a man and bought men with Your precious blood? And will You not come to them and press them to Your bosom and make them Thine?" As the brother calls on God, he appears to come close to Him and lay hold upon Him, and say, "I beseech You, have mercy upon my fellow men."

There is something blessed in each of those prayers. I do not know which I prefer, but I do know that when I can get the blending of the prayers—the awe and the holy boldness and the familiarity and the sense of sovereignty—I find an amazing sweetness fill my heart. Did you ever hear a prayer of that kind that moved the Lord's heart in the wilderness? I refer to the prayer of Moses, when he said, "If not, blot me, I pray thee, out of thy book which thou hast written" (Ex. 32:32). This is the prayer of self-sacrifice, when the man feels, "I would pawn my soul to have these people saved; I would lose myself if but this nation might be redeemed." That is grand praying—not everyone can rise to it. If that were the only prayer spoken, it might grow monotonous, for it lacks compass. But if you put all these prayers together—the prayers of the tender and the brave, the prayers of the awestruck and the familiar, the prayers of the importunate and the self-sacrificing—they fill the golden bowl full of sweet odors.

For my part, I love at prayer meetings to hear the prayers of the aged. Our church prayer meetings have lacked recently through the loss of one dear saint whose prayers used to be marrow and fatness to some of our souls. The prayers of believers on the verge of heaven are to us as angels to lead us also up to the gates of pearl. It is very pleasant to hear the prayers of young people also, even the very young, for as they talk before the Lord there is a charming simplicity and frankness too seldom found in others. And then, the prayers of those in middle life, full of pressing trouble and overflowing with joy, have their peculiar aroma. I believe God loves to see them all mixed in the golden bowls.

What if I add that God would have His people with their various peculiarities put their prayers together? I, as a Calvinist, remark that our Armenian friends pray wonderfully. I can seldom perceive much difference between them and ourselves, but no doubt we view particular parts of the truth differently. Now these various constitutions of Christians affect in some degree their prayers, and when they are blended, they give a peculiar harmony of sweetness to the incense.

It is also delightful to think that the prayers of different nationalities are being put into the golden bowl. Our French brethren always charm me when they pray. There is a tender, filial love, an affectionate gentleness that is most delicious. Our American friends, so bold and sanguine, also delight us with their confidence in God. Their prayers will balance somewhat the timidity of the French utterance. Then our German brethren, with their deep thoughtfulness and their habit of going to the bottom of things, how solidly they make supplication. So with all our brethren of many lands. What a choice amalgam they make! I have been present at prayer meetings when I have heard the various nations pray, and my heart has rejoiced. I believe that to God there is a peculiar harmony in the blending prayers of the many peoples and tongues.

Look back and think of the prayers of all the ages as being in the golden bowl at this one time. The prayers of the apostles, the cries of the persecuted times, the wrestlings of the lonely ones of the Middle Ages, the moans from the valleys and mountains of Piedmont, the pleadings of Reformers and Puritans—all in the golden bowl together, and all with the live coals upon them, coming up from the hand of the great covenant Angel who stands for them before the throne, pleading with God on the behalf of His people. Let us rejoice that the blended prayers of the church are very sweet to the Eternal God.

Let Us Blend Our Prayers

If united prayer is sweet to God, let us give Him much of it. We cannot make God happier than He is in reality, for He is the infinitely happy God. Yet, if there is anything concerning which He expresses satisfaction, let us abound in it. O church of God, cry day and night to Him. If your voice, O spouse, is sweet in His ears, turn not away your face and let not your voice be silent. But cry, and even in the night watches, pour out your heart like water before the Lord God.

I am afraid we fail very much in devotion because we do not value it correctly. I believe the sermon is a very important part of devotion, but I do not believe that it is the all-important matter. I have heard friends speak as if our praying and singing were only a preliminary affair to be gotten through. But praying is the end of preaching. The preaching is only the stalk, while the real ear is the devotion that we pray to God. Let us see to this, and seeing God is pleased with prayer, offer it to Him more and more. And remember that if we do so, we shall find a blessing in it ourselves. The more we pray, the more we shall want to pray. The more we pray, the more we can pray. The more we pray, the more we shall pray. He who prays little will pray less, but he who prays much will pray more. And remember that prayer is effectual with God. We want to see souls saved. Are we not getting weary of living in this world among so many who are going to hell? Is it not terrible to think that after all the church is doing, thousands are being lost every day? We ought to bestir ourselves for men's souls, and we cannot do better for them than by praying for them. Let us, therefore, bestir ourselves in prayer.

In the eighth chapter of the Revelation, you will find that the great angel who stood before God with the golden censer in his hand, full of the prayers of the saints, held it up, and the smoke went up to God. But after a while, when the incense was all burnt out, he took the golden censer and filled it with coals from off the altar, and when he emptied the golden censer out upon the earth, there were voices and thunders and lightnings and earthquakes. Now when the censer of God's church shall have been well filled with prayer and that prayer shall have been presented to the Lord, He will begin to work. And the censer that has been a weapon before God to prevail with Him shall then become against men a weapon to prevail with them. God will fill it full of coals and pour it out upon the earth. His divine power shall then be seen. Then will come voices—preachers here and there rise, voices denouncing oppression, voices crying against false religion, voices preaching truth, voices declaring Christ. Then will come thunderings, for with the Gospel will go the voice of God, which thunders louder than the voice of man. Then will flash forth lightnings, for the light of God's power and truth will come forth with majesty, and men's hearts shall be smitten with it and made obedient to it. And then shall earthquakes shake society, till the thrones of despots reel, till hoary customs are dashed in pieces, till the land that could not be plowed with the Gospel shall be broken up with secret heavings from the Eternal God.

We have only to pray. All things are possible to us. Pray. You have the key in the door of heaven—keep it there and turn it till the gate shall open. Pray, for prayer holds the chain that binds the old dragon. Prayer can hold fast and restrain even Satan himself. Pray. God girds you with omnipotence if you know how to pray. May we not fail here, but may the Spirit of God strengthen us, and to God shall be the glory forever and ever.